DISCLAIMER

This book is a BASIC guide only. It serves as an introduction to car maintenance. It will explain terms and help you understand what is under the bonnet of your car. It will enable you to ask more intelligent questions when you meet with your mechanic. This book is not meant to be a replacement for professional advice. ALWAYS seek the assistance of a qualified professional before proceeding. In no event will the author be liable to you or anyone else for any loss or damage resulting from reliance on the information in this book or for any consequential loss or damage.

essential
CarCare
for girls

Everything a girl needs to know about
taking care of her car

Danielle McCormick

First published as *The Essential Guide to Car Care for Girls* in 2007 by RTB Media, Republic of Ireland

Essential Car Care for Girls published by RTB Media in 2008
Registered Offices:
7 Vernon Court,
Clontarf,
Dublin 3,
Ireland.

ISBN 978-0-9557329-1-1

Designed and typeset by **Susan Meaney (www.smeaney.com)**
Printed by **Bookwell**

Acknowledgements:
Design: Susan Meaney, Blanca Fons Vicedo. Illustrations: Shane Christopher, Paul O'Donnell. Copy Editing: Catherine Best. Photography: Louise Daly. Art Direction: Denise Kinsella. Female Model: Elizabeth Dempsey. Male Model: David Fox. Consulting Mechanics: Dermott Lee, John French.

With thanks to the following for their kind contributions along the way – Noelle Moran, Jenny Boyce, Brian McConnell, Tom and Jamie McCormick.

A complete catalogue record for this book can be obtained from the British Library on request.

A word from the author

Isn't it amazing that in an era when no one would bat an eyelid at a female prime minister, president, army officer or doctor, the thought of a woman confidently changing the tyre of her car would be laughed at?

The common belief is that when it comes to cars, women should just leave it to the men. But why should that be? Anyone who went to school with boys will know that we girls are just as capable as they are, if not more so. What's more, the notion of "leaving it to the men" also assumes every woman who has a car also has a reliable man in her life...

Your car is a piece of machinery, and like most machinery there are things you are supposed to do to it along the way to make sure it works properly. You wouldn't get into an aircraft that hadn't been regularly checked by an engineer, would you? Yet every day millions of women get into cars that haven't had any maintenance carried out in years! By the time smoke is coming out of your engine you have probably done a lot of expensive damage and significantly reduced the amount of money you will get for the car when it comes to sell it on.

Knowing what to do to look after your car is not hard. Like anything in life, the information is all there, you just need to know how to find it. **Essential Car Care for Girls** has been designed to teach a woman everything she needs to know about her set of wheels.

I recommend that you read through the book once so you learn all about your car and the things you have to do to keep it in prime condition. Then stash the book in your glove box so it will be right there when you need it and you don't have to go running to find a man!

Contents

Section 1
HOW YOUR CAR WORKS

Have you ever thought that something was really hard and "no⁺ for you" and then had to try your hand at it and realised it was actually quite easy? It is probably the same for learning how your car works. If boys can understand it, then there is absolutely no reason why a girl shouldn't be able to!

Understanding how your car actually works, from the time you put your key into the ignition to when your wheels begin to turn, is a fascinating journey. Knowing what happens under your bonnet and how all the components make your car move should mean that the next time you have to take your car to a mechanic you will understand what he is talking about.

Once you know how your car works, then understanding the car lingo should be no problem!

LET'S GET STARTED...

When the automobile was first invented there was such excitement about this amazing piece of machinery that could transport people long distances in great comfort. However now cars have become such an ingrained part of our everyday life that we take them completely for granted. When you are sitting in your car you are sitting in a highly sophisticated piece of machinery but you may have no clue as to how anything inside it works!

We tend to care more about things when we understand them, so hopefully when you appreciate how all the different parts of your car are working for you, you will return the favour and give your car the ongoing TLC it deserves.

There are thousands of different makes and models of cars on our roads today. The majority of modern cars are based around the same type of engine, but each model will have slight variations on how all the components work together compared to another model. In order to explain to you how your car works we are going to describe how a "typical" engine works.

From the time you turn your key in the ignition to the moment when your wheels actually start turning there are lots of different processes happening at great speed. Before we go through a description of the process from start to finish, there is one place that is worth looking at in more detail because this is where all the action takes place – **the cylinders.**

Some wonderful scientists discovered that if you add a tiny amount of high energy fuel (such as petrol) to a larger volume of air (roughly 1 part petrol to 14 parts air) you can create a very useful gas. When this gas is put in a small enclosed space and ignited, it releases an incredible amount of energy. Then some exceptionally clever scientists discovered that they could use this energy in a useful way to get machines to carry us around. The next thing you know, the noble horse was out of a job and the automobile came into being.

THE MAIN COMPONENTS YOU NEED TO UNDERSTAND INSIDE THE CYLINDER ARE:

1. **The piston** – a sliding piece of metal that moves up and down inside the cylinder.

2. **The intake valve** – the part of the cylinder that allows the air-fuel mix inside the chamber.

3. **The exhaust valve** – the part of the cylinder that releases the exhaust (used) fumes from the chamber.

4. **Internal combustion chamber** – the enclosed space created when the pistons move down the cylinder, which contains the explosions made by the ignited fuel.

5. **The spark plug** – produces the spark which ignites the air-fuel mix.

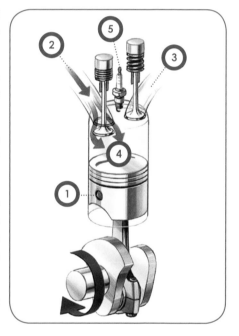

Almost all of today's modern car engines use what is known as a **four-stroke combustion cycle** to create movement. To put it in simpler terms, there are four movements which happen in a particular order. These movements consume fuel and result in the release of a useful energy.

FOUR-STROKE COMBUSTION CYCLE

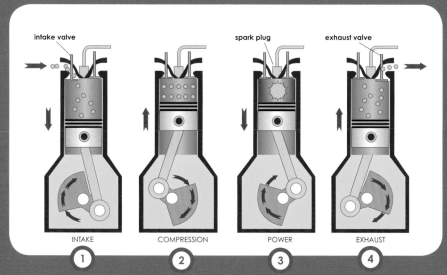

1. The first stroke is known as the **intake or induction stroke.** The cycle begins with the piston at the top of the cylinder. The intake valve opens and the piston moves down the cylinder allowing the air-fuel mix to enter the open space.

2. Next is the **compression stroke**. The piston now moves back up towards the top of the cylinder thereby squeezing the air-fuel mix into a smaller space (i.e. compression). This will ultimately make the explosion more powerful.

3. When the piston has reached the highest point in the cylinder that it can go, the spark plug emits a spark which ignites the air-fuel mix causing an explosion. The power of this explosion pushes the piston back down the cylinder with great force. The bottom of the pistons is attached at right angles to a shaft with offset bearings called a **crankshaft**. The up-and-down motion of the pistons in this cycle rotate the crankshaft in a similar way to the up-and-down motion of your legs on a bicycle. Ultimately, the motion that comes out of the engine is rotational which, funnily enough, is exactly the motion needed to turn the wheels of a car! This rotational force is known as **torque.**

4. Finally, after the explosion, the exhaust valve opens and the piston moves back up to the top of the cylinder, forcing the exhaust fumes out of the exhaust valve. Now that it is at the top of the cylinder it is ready to start the cycle again.

REVOLUTIONS PER MINUTE

In a car engine this cycle repeats itself inside each cylinder thousands of times a minute. This is where the expression "Revs (or revolutions) per minute" comes from. Your **rev counter** is telling you how many thousand times per minute these explosions are turning the crankshaft. Next time you are driving check out your rev counter and see how hard your engine is working for you!

V-shaped cylinder bank

CYLINDER BANKS

There are a number of cylinders in your engine. The number you have depends on what type of car you have. The cylinders can be arranged in various different shapes: "in-line" means they are arranged in a row; "V" means they are arranged in two banks (rows) in a "V" shape; "flat" means there are two opposing banks but in a flat shape. When someone says they have a "V6" or "V8" engine, it means there are 6 or 8 cylinders arranged in a V shape.

And there you have it. Now that you have a basic understanding of how energy is created to move the vehicle, let's look at the process fully so you'll have a better knowledge of how all the other parts of your engine are working together to make your car move.

WHAT HAPPENS WHEN I TURN THE KEY IN THE IGNITION?

When you turn the key in the ignition, the **battery** powers the **starter motor**, which begins to turn the crankshaft to get the pistons moving.

Air then enters your engine via a filter which removes any dirt or grit from the incoming air. At this point fuel (either petrol or diesel) is added to the air to create a vapourised gas. This gas is now waiting in a chamber for you to decide how much of it goes into the engine. The amount of gas going into your engine is controlled by your foot on the accelerator pedal. If you want to add more fuel to your engine (to go fast or climb a hill) you must press the accelerator pedal down as far as it can go. This opens the **throttle valves** wide allowing large amounts of gas through. If you only need a little bit of power (and therefore fuel) you will put your foot down lightly on the pedal, which will just open the throttle valve a fraction.

From here the gas goes through what is called an **intake manifold,** which essentially distributes the gas through a series of passages to each of the cylinders through **valves**. The opening and closing of these valves is carried out by the **camshaft.**

In most cars, when air enters the engine (to be mixed with fuel) the way it comes in is the way it is used. In some cars however, the air is pressurised so more air-fuel mix can be squeezed into the cylinder to increase performance. This is referred to as **turbo charged** or **turbo-boost.**

NOW WE COME TO THE CYLINDER BIT

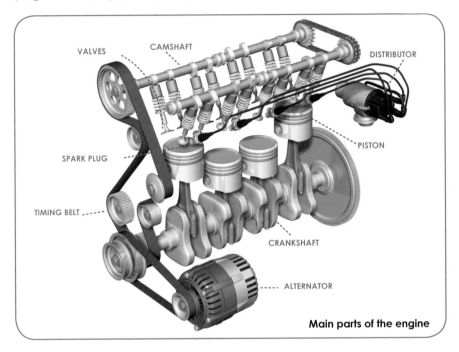

Main parts of the engine

The gas then enters each cylinder via the **intake valve**. The piston comes up to the top of the cylinder and at this point the valves are closed.

At the exact same time the **distributor** causes a spark to go to the **spark plug**, which ignites the fuel in the cylinder, causing an explosion. The explosions that occur inside the different cylinders are timed to go off at different intervals ensuring the crankshaft is continually being spun. The force of the explosion pushes the piston down the cylinder sharply. The pistons are attached at a right angle to the **crankshaft**. As the piston is forced down it causes the crankshaft to rotate.

So now your pistons are making the crankshaft rotate rapidly. Before all this motion goes to your wheels you need to be able to control it (so your car doesn't go 100 miles an hour when you only need to go 30), therefore the crankshaft goes through a section called the **transmission**. This section of the car is in charge of controlling the power contained in the crankshaft before it goes to the wheels.

The transmission controls the speed/power of your car by providing you with different speed/power ratios otherwise known as gears. For example, in first gear you need a lot of power to initially get your car moving, but you don't need a lot of speed. In a higher gear, the same amount of power would get you a higher speed. The transmission is responsible for regulating all of this. If you have a manual car, you control it with your gear stick.

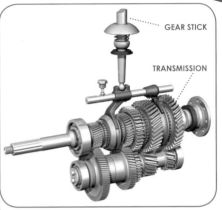

GEAR STICK

TRANSMISSION

The crankshaft is not permanently connected to the transmission. You connect it to the transmission when you engage the clutch. This is why when you have your car in neutral, your engine is running but the wheels don't turn.

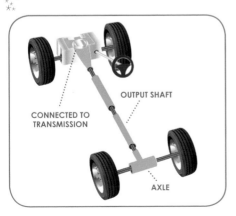

OUTPUT SHAFT

CONNECTED TO TRANSMISSION

AXLE

The transmission is connected to the **output shaft** which is connected to **axles** which are in turn connected to the wheels. When the transmission turns the output shaft this turns the axles which in turn rotates your wheels. Et voilà – you're moving!

Now you know how all the main engine parts are working to make your car move it's time to look at the other vital components.

ELECTRONIC CONTROL UNIT (ECU)

In recent years cars have become much more high-tech and now even have computers in them programming certain elements of your engine. The Electronic Control Unit (ECU) controls lots of things such as the fuel injection system, air-conditioning, air-flow and idling speeds, e.g. when you are sitting in traffic. In some instances, when you bring your car to your mechanic or dealership they will be able to plug a laptop into your car and get readings of how all the different components attached to the system are working.

The ECU is also sometimes referred to as "the brains".

OIL

There are lots of moving parts in your engine and oil makes sure that all parts are lubricated so they can move easily.

The main parts that need oil are:

1. **The pistons** – so they can slide up and down the cylinders.

2. **The camshaft and the crankshaft** – they have bearings which enable them to move freely and oil is used on these bearings to help them move.

Usually oil is sucked out of the oil pan by a pump which then passes it through a filter to remove any dirt. The oil is then squirted under high pressure onto the bearings and the cylinder walls. The oil then trickles down into an area called **the sump**, where it is collected. The process then starts all over again.

ALTERNATOR

The alternator is an important player in the electrical system of your car.

When the battery has started your car engine there is a belt within your engine that begins to rotate. The movement of this belt drives a device known as the alternator. The alternator produces electricity by converting mechanical energy into electrical energy.

This electrical energy is used to power all the electrical consumers in your car such as the ignition lights, heater, wipers, radio, etc. It also puts back into the battery the energy that the starter motor has used.

REGULATOR

This is a device that regulates the amount of energy in the alternator to ensure it has just the right amount of energy it needs.

DISTRIBUTOR

DISTRIBUTOR

The distributor gets the **ignition coil** to generate a spark at the precise instant that it is needed. It is also responsible for directing (i.e. distributing) that spark to the right cylinder at the right time. It has to do this at exactly the right instant and up to several thousand times a minute for each cylinder in the engine. If the timing spark is off by even a fraction of a second the engine will run poorly or not at all.

The distributor is now being replaced in more modern engines with the **distributorless ignition system** or **separate coil packs**. These provide the same function as the distributor except they are electronically controlled by sensors.

TIMING BELT

The camshaft (at the top of the cylinder) and crankshaft (at the bottom of the cylinder) need to work in synchronisation. The timing belt is a belt which is connected between the two, ensuring that they work in time with each other.

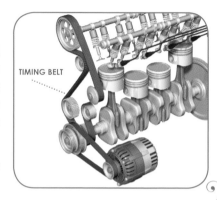

TIMING BELT

 Consult your **owner's manual** to find out how often your timing belt needs to be changed.

> Depending on the model of your car, timing belts usually need to be replaced every 60,000–100,000 miles.

CAR RADIATOR

COOLING SYSTEM

With all the fuel being burnt, as you can imagine, the engine will get quite hot! As a result, your car has a cooling system which keeps the temperature of the engine down. The cooling system mainly consists of the **radiator**, **water pump** and **temperature gauge**. Water circulates through passages around the cylinders and then travels through the radiators to cool down.

EXHAUST SYSTEM

Remember when the gas was burned in the combustion chamber? As soon as it has been burnt it exits the combustion chamber via an **exhaust valve** and enters an exhaust system.

Most modern cars have a **catalytic converter** in their exhaust system which burns off any unused fuel and certain chemicals before it is released from the car via the **exhaust pipe**. The catalytic converter minimises the amount of toxic fumes coming from your car.

HEAD GASKET

The **head gasket** is tucked away inside your engine so it's not something that you see when you open up your bonnet, but if it blows you can expect a big bill from your mechanic!

WHAT IS IT AND WHY DO I NEED TO WORRY?

The **cylinder head** (the block that seals all the tops of your cylinders) is made in one part of the car factory and the **engine block** (which contains all the main bodies of the cylinders) is made in another part of the factory. When it comes to putting your engine together these two pieces need to fit seamlessly together. With all the explosions taking place inside the cylinders there is no room for cracks or open spaces! So, in order to ensure the cylinder head and engine block fit seamlessly together the car people put a piece of metal called a head gasket in between them.

If your engine overheats for a sustained amount of time the head gasket can warp or crack and eventually blow. Replacing a head gasket is very labour-intensive and therefore very costly. That is why it is really important that as soon as your engine shows any sign of overheating, you should pull over as soon as it is safe to do so and call for roadside assistance. It is generally much cheaper to call for roadside assistance than to replace a head gasket.

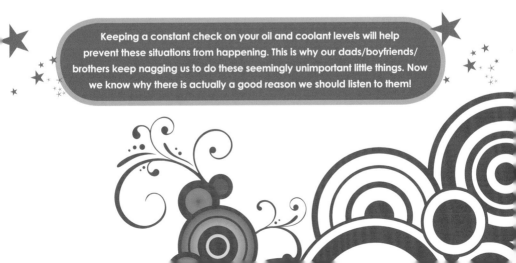

Keeping a constant check on your oil and coolant levels will help prevent these situations from happening. This is why our dads/boyfriends/ brothers keep nagging us to do these seemingly unimportant little things. Now we know why there is actually a good reason we should listen to them!

FILTERS

There are lots of moving liquids and gases in your car. Filters are set in strategic places along each system to catch and trap anything that might contaminate it. Your car has several types of filters such as an **oil filter**, an **air filter** and a **fuel filter.**

These need to be changed quite regularly and your mechanic should do this for you during your services.

BELTS AND HOSES

Your car has various belts which are used for rotating different components in your engine e.g. **fan belt, alternator belt.**

Hoses transport fluid or gases from one part of the engine to another. If a belt cracks or a hose gets a hole in it, it can severely affect the performance of your engine.

WHAT IS THE DIFFERENCE BETWEEN A DIESEL AND A PETROL ENGINE?

Diesel and petrol cars are basically the same but the main difference between the two is how the explosions that take place in the cylinders occur. In a petrol engine, fuel is mixed with air and then it is forced into the cylinders where this air-fuel mix is compressed by the pistons and ignited by sparks from spark plugs.

However, in a diesel engine, the air is compressed **before** the fuel is added to it. When air is compressed it heats up. So, by the time the fuel is added to the compressed air it is very hot so the air-fuel mix ignites automatically. There is no need for a spark plug to create a spark. So, in short, in a petrol engine a spark plug ignites the explosion in the cylinders, whereas in a diesel engine pressure causes the ignition.

Now that you know what all the different parts of your engine do, let's see where they are when you open your bonnet. Not all car engines are the same so be aware that the parts of your engine might be arranged slightly differently.

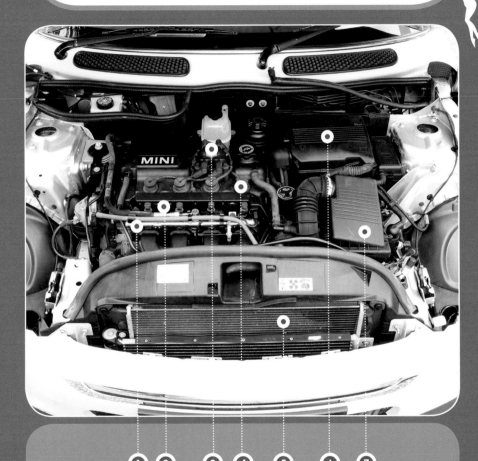

1) INTAKE MANIFOLD

2) CYLINDERS

3) ELECTRONIC CONTROL UNIT

4) SPARK PLUGS

5) RADIATOR

6) BATTERY

7) AIR FILTER

BRAKES

There are usually two different types of brakes in your car; **disc brakes** and **drum brakes**. Disc brakes work in a very similar way to the brakes on a bicycle. On a bicycle there is a piece called a **caliper** which squeezes the brake pads against the wheel. In a car the disc brakes have a caliper (guarded with brake pads) which grabs onto the **disc** of the wheels to get them to stop. Drum brakes work on the same principles as disc brakes. However, a drum brake presses against the inside of the drum.

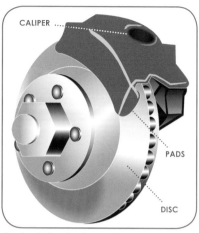

Typical disc brake system

The force that is used to get the brake pads to work is transmitted hydraulically, i.e. through a fluid. When you step on your brake pedal you are actually pushing against a plunger which forces brake fluid through a series of tubes and hoses. This ultimately puts pressure on the brake pads to stop your wheels.

The brake pads wear down over time and need to be replaced quite regularly. If you hear noises when your car is braking it's time to take it to your mechanic!

SUSPENSION SYSTEM

Have you ever bounced a ball on the ground and it hit a stone? You may remember that the stone caused the ball to go in a completely different direction to the way you wanted it to go. Similarly, without a **suspension system** in your car every time your tyres hit a stone or a bump it would send the tyres off in the wrong direction. This would make the car difficult to steer and uncomfortable for any passengers. For this reason your car has a suspension system which has been designed to counteract the effects of hitting imperfections in the road.

The suspension system is made up of **springs** and **shock absorbers**. The main body of the car is attached to the base of the car by springs. These springs absorb any of the "bouncing" energy so the frame and body of the car remain undisturbed as you drive.

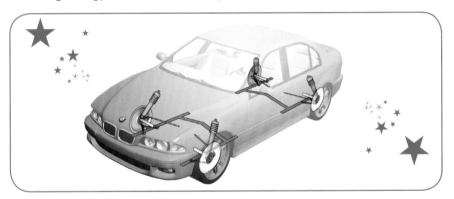

SHOCK ABSORBERS

If the spring in the suspension system was left to its own devices it would bounce up and down until it ran out of energy, which wouldn't be very pleasant for anybody sitting in the car. A shock absorber is a device that absorbs the energy from the springs to stop the bouncing motion.

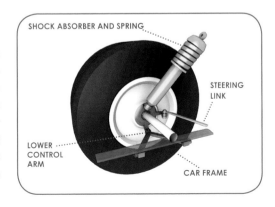

SHOCK ABSORBER AND SPRING

STEERING LINK

LOWER CONTROL ARM

CAR FRAME

TYRES

As the tyre is the part of the car that actually connects with the road it plays a vital, but often overlooked, role.

Tyres are made of rubber and have a tube in the middle of them. If it gets damaged the tube deflates and you have a flat tyre! The rubber and tubing create a soft ride for you and are also part of your suspension system.

In order to grip the surface of the ground, tyres have a tread cut into their surface. With all the friction caused by rotating at great speed along the road, the tread in the tyre wears down. If the tread becomes too thin it inhibits the ability of the tyre to grip onto the road, which can cause accidents. This is why in most countries it is now a legal requirement that the tread of the tyre must not get to less than 1.6mm.

TYPES OF TYRE

There are a few different types of tyre available on the market today.

Standard tyres
The most common tyres have thick rubber with a steel **rim** (the piece of metal that supports the rubber tyre) and a **hubcap** (a wheel cover that fits over the hub of the wheel).

Rubber tyre

Tyre tread

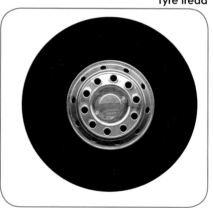

Standard tyre

Alloy wheels

Alloy wheels

Alloy wheels are made of an alloy (two metals mixed together) based on either aluminium or magnesium. They tend to be lighter than the standard wheels which helps improve steering and speed.

Low-profile tyres

Low-profile tyres

Low-profile tyres have a very thin tyre base. This lowers the distance of the main body of the car to the ground which makes them looks sportier and gives them a better grip to the ground. Although with less air in the tyres you will feel every bump!

These tyres tend to be more expensive and don't last as long as standard tyres but they help the car handle the roads better at higher speeds so are a favourite with speed demons.

Run-flats

Run-flats

Some luxury and sports cars are now coming with run-flat tyres. Run-flats contain a sensor which detects any loss of pressure and relays this message to the dashboard in the event of a flat. They have reinforcements built into them so that you will have enough time to drive to the nearest garage without having to change the tyre yourself. The downside of run-flats is that they have to be replaced with another run-flat tyre, and they are more expensive than standard tyres.

Section 2

GETTING DOWN WITH THE LINGO

Sometimes it can feel that when people are talking about cars it is as if they are speaking another language. They talk excitedly to you about their new "3 litre V6 TDI coupé with 240 horsepower" like you know exactly what they are talking about – when the truth is you haven't got a clue. After reading this section, though, you should be able to talk with confidence to even the biggest car enthusiast.

PERFORMANCE CHARACTERISTICS

WHAT EXACTLY DOES LITRE SIZE MEAN?

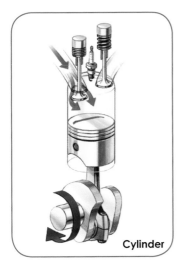

Cylinder

If you can remember back to your days in science class, cylinders typically held liquids and the units we use to measure liquids are litres. Similarly in the cylinders in your car, the space that is available for the air-fuel mix to fill is also measured in litres. The more space you have available, the more air-fuel mix you can get in, which ultimately means more power.

One cylinder might have ½ litre of space available for the air-fuel mix. But remember, your car usually has a number of cylinders so if you had 6 cylinders with ½ litre space available in each = 6 x 0.5 = 3 litres. This measurement is sometimes called the **engine displacement.**

A very small economy-sized car might only have small cylinders which in total amount to 1 litre, whereas a high-performance car like a Ferrari's cylinders might add up to 6 litres.

Having a large-sized engine might sound impressive, but the bigger the size of engine you have the more fuel you will need to run it. The running costs of cars with big engines can be very expensive!

VALVES

Each cylinder in the engine has valves; valves that allow the air-fuel mix into the cylinder and valves that allow the exhaust fumes out. The minimum a cylinder requires is two – one for each function. Some car engineers design the cylinders to have more than the standard two valves as this enables more air-fuel mix to enter the cylinders. If a car has four cylinders with four valves in each you would say it has a "4 cylinder, 16 valve engine"

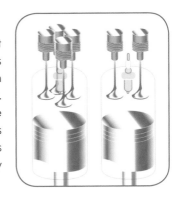

HORSEPOWER (hp)

There is no doubting that even the biggest car enthusiast would struggle to have a firm grip on horsepower and its exact definition – so rather than confusing you with lots of numbers and calculations here is an overview of what it is so that if you hear it in conversation, you will have some sort of idea what people are talking about.

History of Horsepower

Just think back to an old movie – set in a time before they had cars – when horses were used a lot in heavy lifting and transporting people around. So, back in the day, when famous scientist James Watt (yes, the same guy written on your light bulb!) was trying to convince people of the amazing powers of the new steam engine the best way he could do it was compare the power of the new engine to the power of a horse.

James Watt came up with a calculation that one horse could do 30,000 foot pounds of work in one minute. It is not exactly a straightforward measurement that is easy to understand but for some reason it has stuck as a measurement for calculating the power of engines – including the car.

Unless you are a car engineer there is no need to be a pro at horsepower. For most people it is just enough to understand that it is a way of measuring the power of a car and in terms of horsepower to know what is relatively good and what is relatively poor.

The table below highlights the horsepower of some well-known cars which are a good benchmark for comparing your car against.

	Car	Weight	Horsepower
	Ford Focus	2,470 lbs	136
	Porsche	2,975 lbs	300
	Ferrari Enzo	3,009 lbs	650
	Formula 1 car	1,323 lbs	900

You will notice in the above chart that the weight of the car is included. This is because if you had two cars with the same horsepower but one weighs twice as much as the other, the heavier car wouldn't be as fast as the lighter one. When racing cars are competing against each other for speed they try and get the highest horsepower they can and build the cars as light as they can. That is why racing cars only have one seat. Everything is geared to keeping the weight of the car down.

BRAKE HORSEPOWER (bhp)

Brake horsepower is the measurement of the car's horsepower when it comes straight out of the crankshaft. It loses some of its power when it goes through the gearbox and other components so the actual horsepower that is delivered to the wheels tends to be a lower figure than the bhp which is produced from the engine.

TORQUE

The energy that moves through your car is rotational and torque is a measurement used to gauge a force that occurs in a twisting motion. It is calculated in foot pounds (ft–lbs) and is another way of measuring the power of the car.

ZERO TO 60

Sometimes in car talk you hear the expression "It does zero to 60" in X amount of seconds. Cars come in all shapes and sizes and with different engines so it can be hard to compare one against the other. The "zero to 60" method has become a way of comparing two different cars' acceleration. It is a way of saying how many seconds it takes one car to get from a starting position (i.e. zero miles per hour) to 60 miles per hour. For example a Ford Ka can get from zero to 60 in 11.8 seconds whereas a Ferrari can go from zero to 60 in 3.3 seconds.

In the metric system it is measured in 0–100 kilometres an hour.

LITRES PER 100 KILOMETRES

Litres per 100 Kilometres refers to how many litres of petrol your car needs to take you 100km. The less petrol you need, the more fuel efficient your car is.

Type of car	Litres per 100 Kilometres
Lamborghini	28
Toyota Corolla	8.5
Toyota Prius	5

As you will see from the chart above having a fancy sports car may be all very well and good but your petrol costs will be very expensive. On the other hand the new hybrid cars should cost very little to run. In a year if a Lamborghini was to do the same amount of miles as a hybrid car, the Lamborghini owner's petrol bill would be nearly six times as much as the hybrid's. That's given you something to think about next time you are buying a car!

ENGINE FEATURES

TURBOCHARGER

In cars ideally you want to try and get as much power out of your engine as you can. One way of doing this is by packing as much of the air-fuel mix into the cylinders of the engine as possible. A turbocharger is a device which uses the pressure from the exhaust to create more pressure in the cylinders so that they can receive more of the air-fuel mix.

TURBO

If a car is described as being a "Turbo" it means it has a turbocharger in its engine.

TWIN TURBO

"Twin Turbo" means that the car has two turbochargers. Each turbocharger is driven by one half of the exhaust system. If the car has two exhaust pipes then a turbocharger would be connected to each one.

SUPERCHARGER

A supercharger performs the same function as the turbocharger inasmuch as it increases the amount of air-fuel mix the cylinders can take. While the turbocharger is run from the pressure of the exhaust system a supercharger gets its power from a belt or can sometimes be attached to the engine's crankshaft. A supercharger is something that can be added on to a car after you have purchased it and is an inexpensive way of increasing the power of the engine.

CARBURETTOR

The carburettor is a device which mixes the fuel and the air before it is passed on to the engine for combustion. They are simple, non-computerised devices but they have generally been replaced in cars since the 1980s by the more efficient fuel-injection system.

FUEL-INJECTION SYSTEM

More modern cars now have a computerised system which mixes the air-fuel mix before it goes into the engine. This is called a Fuel-Injection System. Because it is computerised it is considered to be more efficient than its predecessor, the carburettor, making sure the correct mix is put in every time.

TDI

TDI stands for Turbo Direct Injection.

TDI is something that is just found on a diesel engine. It used to be the norm that in diesel cars, the air-fuel mix would have to go to a pre-combustion chamber before it was sent to the main cylinders of the engine. However, in a TDI car the fuel is directly injected.

A TDI car also has a turbocharger. With both direct injection and a turbocharger it makes for a more powerful car.

GTi

GTi is an expression coined by car engineers. It stands for Gran Tourismo injection or Grand Tourisme injection. It comes from the word Grand Tourer which has become synonymous with describing high-powered sports cars that have been designed to race long distances. The "Injection" part means that it has fuel injection as opposed to a carburettor.

DRIVING CHARACTERISTICS

CAR HANDLING

Car handling refers to how responsive the car is to your steering. If you are trying to drive around a corner and your car seems to go a different way to the way you want, then you would say the car doesn't have good handling. If you are driving around a corner at a very fast speed and your car still does what you want it to then you would say the car has great handling. It can also refer to when you are driving in a straight line. If you are keeping your steering wheel straight and your car keeps on swerving in a different direction then this is a sign of poor car handling.

UNDERSTEER

If you are approaching a corner and the steering wheel doesn't turn the wheels as much as you want, then this is said to be understeer.

OVERSTEER

If you are turning a corner and the rear wheels do not follow the front wheels and instead veer towards the outside of the turn, this is known as oversteer. This can sometimes lead to your car spinning which is quite dangerous.

TRACTION

This refers to how well the tyres grip to the ground. New tyres with a deep tread tend to have good traction. Old tyres which are worn and have very little tread left would have poor traction.

REAR WHEEL DRIVE (RWD)

In a Rear Wheel Drive car the power created from the engine is distributed to the rear wheels and these in turn drive the car. RWD tends to be a feature found in high-performance cars because it makes the car handle better in dry conditions. This means drivers can turn corners at greater speeds than in a normal car. It also offers better braking ability.

RWD is more expensive to put in place so a lot of the mass-produced cars have front wheel drive.

FRONT WHEEL DRIVE

When the engine only drives the front wheels of the car.

FOUR WHEEL DRIVE

Also known as 4 x 4. This describes when the engine powers all four wheels.

ABS

"Anti-Lock Brakes" or "Anti-Locking Brake System". When you have to brake suddenly it is usually because there is an emergency and it is the moment you need your brakes the most. Some brake systems used to "lock" at the moment of greatest need so car manufacturers developed a way of stopping the brakes from locking in these situations.

POWER STEERING

It used to take a lot more effort to turn the wheels of the car from the steering wheel before they invented power steering. If a car has a power steering system it means that there is a separate power source that is helping it to turn the wheels.

AUTOMATIC

If a car is described as an "automatic" it means that it has an automatic transmission or gearbox. The transmission will automatically shift the gears as it accelerates and decelerates so the driver does not need to keep on changing the gears manually. Typically the functions of an automatic gear stick are "Park", "Drive" and "Reverse".

MANUAL

A manual car is a car in which the driver physically changes the gears up and down themselves. A manual transmission allows the driver to decide when they want the car to go into a higher or lower gear, giving them more control.

TYPES OF CAR

SPORTS CAR

There is a lot of debate amongst car enthusiasts as to the correct definition of a "sports car". The hard-core enthusiasts would say that a sports car must be a car that has been built solely for performance rather than practicality. These cars tend to be built for speed rather than family use so only have two seats, are quite low and have aerodynamic bodies. These are usually made by specialist sports car manufacturers such as Ferrari, Porsche and Lamborghini.

HIGH-PERFORMANCE CAR

Mass market manufacturers such as BMW, Mercedes and Ford have begun to bring out high-performance versions of their existing models which have some of the features of a sports car, such as a more powerful engine or a sleeker look. Some people consider these to be sports cars but the diehard enthusiast would just call them a "high-performance car".

HYBRID CAR

In a normal car a lot of the energy that is created is wasted. When car engineers were trying to make a more fuel-efficient car they began with trying to use the energy that was already being created in the car more efficiently. Hybrid cars usually have a Rechargeable Energy Storage System (RESS) which collects any energy that was wasted or generated by the car itself. For example the braking movement of a car creates a lot of energy so it collects it and puts it back into the car's energy system. The hybrid has sensors in it that automatically shut down the engine whenever it doesn't need to be used, such as when you are sitting in traffic or going down a hill.

ELECTRIC CAR

In an electric car, the car is driven by an electric motor and batteries as opposed to a four-stroke combustion cycle engine. As there is no combustion in the car, it doesn't produce any emissions directly. However, the batteries need to be charged and if they are charged from a building that gets its power from a CO_2-creating source then the car indirectly creates emissions. If the batteries are charged from a renewable source, such as a wind farm, then you can drive a car safe in the knowledge that you are not creating any harmful CO_2 emissions. The disadvantages of electric cars are that they can only travel short distances before the batteries need to be recharged and they aren't as fast as conventional cars.

BIODIESEL

Biodiesel cars use alternative fuels such as oils made from vegetables or animal fats to run diesel engines. The crops that the alternative fuels are made from are renewable. Whilst growing, plants absorb carbon dioxide (CO_2) from the atmosphere and release oxygen. The CO_2 emissions produced by biodiesel cars are said to be carbon neutral as any CO_2 produced is soaked up by the crops currently growing.

CAR BODY STYLES

 **SALOON** or sedan is a car which has 2 front seats and at least 2 rear seats with 4 doors and a separate boot.

 **COUPE** Often the sporty variation of a saloon car. These usually only have 2 doors as opposed to 4. The back seats can be quite close to the front seats.

 **ESTATE** aka a station wagon. It has an extended rear cargo section and the full height of the car extends to the boot allowing for much more storage space.

 **HATCHBACK** These are like an estate but usually have much smaller boot space. The boot can be accessed from the back passenger seats.

 **SUV** aka Sports Utility Vehicle, off-road vehicle, four wheel drive or 4 x 4. A SUV typically has towing capabilities, can go off road and can also carry passengers. There is normally no designated boot space as the boot is directly behind seats.

 **MPV** MPV stands for Multi-Purpose Vehicle. It can refer to a minivan or a people carrier, similar in shape to a van but designed for personal use. Usually for carrying larger numbers of people than a normal car.

 **CONVERTIBLE** aka cabriolet. A car with a foldable or retractable roof.

Section 3
CAR MAINTENANCE

It is more than likely that your car is one of the most expensive purchases you will ever make, so doesn't it make sense to look after it properly?

If you don't look after your car you can expect more expensive trips to the mechanic – usually when you can least afford it – and you are more likely to get a lower resale value on your car.

Basic car maintenance is actually quite simple when you know how. Get into the habit of setting aside a few minutes every fortnight or so and carry out the basic checks in this section.

Before we begin...
OWNER'S MANUAL

Doesn't it sometimes feel like the owner's manual was written by "boys" for "boys"? There are lots of technical words and not a lot of pretty pictures! But don't try and avoid it; your owner's manual is an essential tool to running and maintaining your car. You are not expected to read the manual cover to cover, just refer to the relevant sections when you need them. You may even find that when you do start reading the section on, for example, oil, it is surprisingly easy to understand.

Make sure you keep the owner's manual in a safe place in your car. It is usually designed to fit neatly into your glove compartment, so try and keep it there! It should give you all the basic information from how to open your bonnet to how to change your tyre. Just look up the index on the section you need to get the page reference for whatever you need to know.

If your car has lost its owner's manual, try and get another one for your car's precise make and model. You can get them from your car dealer and many are now available to order online.

SYMBOLS ON YOUR DASHBOARD

Cars are becoming much more sophisticated and in newer cars there tend to be a lot more sensors in various parts relaying information to your dashboard to notify you if something isn't right. You should familiarise yourself with the meaning of your dashboard symbols by consulting your owner's manual. Older cars won't be as good at telling you if something is wrong, so you really have to look after them carefully!

> An orange symbol usually means you have a problem and should probably get it checked at your earliest convenience. A red symbol means you should stop using your car and get it checked by a mechanic immediately.

HERE ARE SOME EXAMPLES OF COMMON SYMBOLS:

 Engine warning: Depending on your make of car this usually means there is a problem somewhere in your engine's management system.

 Oil: If this light shows, check your oil levels immediately. A lack of oil can lead to overheating which can seriously damage your engine.

 Battery: If this light shows it means you are experiencing problems with your battery. It can be one of a number of things:
- Your battery's terminals may need cleaning.
- Your battery is not being charged properly by the alternator.
- Your battery usually has a life of 3.5 years so may be nearing the end of its life and needs replacing.

 Brakes: This indicates that you have a problem somewhere in your brake system. You can check your brake fluids to see if they are low but generally all matters that relate to your brake system should be left to the professionals, so take your car to a mechanic as soon as possible.

 Engine overheating: This symbol means your engine is overheating. Pull over as soon as it is safe to do so and call for roadside assistance.

 ABS: If this light appears on your dashboard it means there is a fault somewhere in your anti-locking brake system and it should be checked by a mechanic as soon as possible.

These are just some of the common symbols on your dashboard. Your car manufacturer may have used some more symbols which communicate problems in the car to you.

MAINTENANCE CHECKS

BEFORE YOU OPEN YOUR BONNET:

1. All under-bonnet checks should be done when the engine is turned off.

2. If the engine has been running for any length of time it is likely there will be areas that are very hot!

3. Read your **owner's manual** safety warnings to see if there are any particular safety stickers you should keep an eye out for.

4. If the engine is running, don't put your hands near any fans or belts.

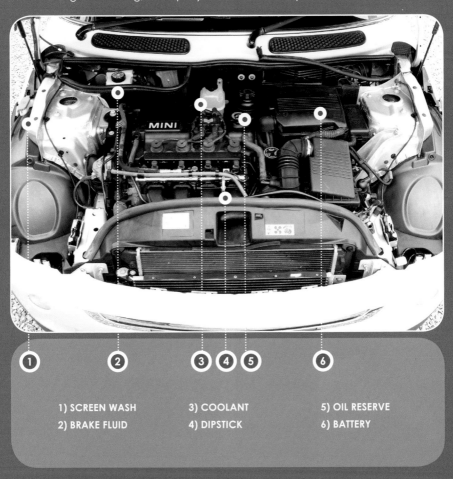

1) SCREEN WASH   3) COOLANT   5) OIL RESERVE
2) BRAKE FLUID   4) DIPSTICK   6) BATTERY

You should check the oil of your car about every two weeks.

CHECKING YOUR OIL

Your car should be stationary for at least five minutes before checking your oil so you can get an accurate oil reading.

A. Locate your dipstick

B. Remove the dipstick

C. Clean it with a rag or paper towel

D. Put the dipstick back in fully for about 5 seconds

E. Remove the dipstick again slowly

F. If the oil level falls below the "min" mark you need to refill

You refill the oil via the oil reserve tank. It usually has a picture of an oil canister on it but if you are unsure of where it is, consult your **owner's manual.**

There are two different types of oil for cars – **synthetic** and **non-synthetic**. Again, consult your owner's manual to see what type your car takes. Most petrol stations and garages will stock both types.

Just because you buy a whole container full of oil doesn't mean you have to put it all in. Stop every now and then when you are refilling and check your oil levels again to make sure you haven't passed the "max" mark.

COOLANT/ANTI-FREEZE

The cooling system of the car is under high pressure and contains fluid that can heat to a higher temperature than boiling water. Therefore, never open or go near the coolant reserve tank or radiator of a car that has just been running.

 Check your **owner's manual** to find out where your coolant reserve tank is located.

It is usually translucent white so you can inspect the fluid levels without opening it. Be careful not to confuse it with the windscreen washer tank, as they look similar.

The reserve tank will have marks on the side of it with "full hot" or "full cold". Remember from science class that when things are hot they expand and when they are cold they contract – hence there are two levels. If your level is below "full cold" when your engine is cold you will need to add fluid until it is near that mark.

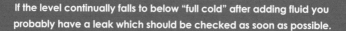

If the level continually falls to below "full cold" after adding fluid you probably have a leak which should be checked as soon as possible.

FULL HOT

FULL COLD

 Check your **owner's manual** to determine the exact fluid you need to add to your cooling system.

BRAKE FLUID

The brake fluid reservoir is under the bonnet, usually in front of the steering wheel.

Most cars today have a transparent reservoir so you can see the level without opening the cover.

Changing brake fluid is something that should be left to the professionals, so in this instance just make sure that the brake fluid levels are above the minimum mark.

If you notice a drop in the levels below the minimum you will need to take your car to a mechanic as it is an indication that there is a fault somewhere in your braking system.

If the level noticeably drops over a short period of time or goes down to about two-thirds full, have your brakes checked as soon as possible.

SCREEN WASH

This may not seem very important but if a big truck has ever splashed mud on your screen on a wet day you will know the importance of having screen wash!

Most modern cars will tell you when your screen wash is running low.

You can buy screen wash or a dilution (which you add to water) at your local petrol station.

Don't be tempted to just put water in! It is important to include a screen wash additive as the additive contains anti-freeze which will stop it from freezing in the winter months. It also has cleaning agents which will help clean your windscreen.

TYRE PRESSURE

WHY IS TYRE PRESSURE IMPORTANT?

Driving with a tyre that is substantially under- or over-inflated can result in tyre failure. This can be dangerous if you're driving fast as you can lose control of the car. The wrong tyre pressure can also mean that the braking capability is dramatically reduced which, if you are driving at speed, can also make you lose control.

Having an under-inflated tyre shortens the life of the tyre and means your car has to work harder. This ultimately uses more fuel unnecessarily – more money: less shopping!

HOW DO I KNOW WHAT MY TYRE PRESSURE SHOULD BE?

You can find out what tyre pressure your car needs by consulting your **owner's manual**. However, sometimes it is written in the glove compartment, driver's door jamb or inside the petrol cap. Some makes of car require different air pressure in the front tyres compared to the back.

Most petrol stations have a tyre pressure gauge in the service area that you can use.

Note: Tyre pressure needs to be checked when the tyres are cold, so ideally check them after a very short journey i.e. from your house to your nearest petrol station.

Door jamb tyre pressure information

Don't forget to check your spare tyre as well. Many a person will tell the sad tale of how they got a flat tyre only to discover their spare had deflated too!

CHECKING YOUR TYRE PRESSURE

- Remove the cap. These can get lost but it should be OK without them.

- Put the top of the pressure gauge around the seal. **(A)**

- Make sure the gauge completely covers all parts of the seal and no air is escaping i.e. there is no hissing sound. **(B)**

- Read the pressure levels. **(C)**

- If the reading on the screen is the same as the one your tyres should have then no further action is required on this tyre. Continue to the next tyre and repeat.

- If the pressure reading you are getting is less than the level it is supposed to be at, you need to add more air. To add more air to your tyres, increase the pressure gauge to the amount required for your tyre. **(D)**

- Return to your tyre and ensure that the gauge completely covers the valve; the system should add the right amount of air to your tyre. **(E)**

- Once you have finished, replace the cap back on the valve (if you can find it!).

A. Put pressure gauge around seal

B. Ensure gauge completely covers all parts of seal

C. Read pressure levels

D. Increase pressure gauge to amount required

E. Return to your tyre and allow gauge to add air

TYRE CONDITION

You should inspect the condition of your tyres every two weeks, while you are checking the air pressure. Look for any excessive wear, cracks, bulging or deep cuts. It is actually illegal to drive with badly damaged tyres.

You also need to check the **tread** on the tyre. The tread is the grooved surface on your tyre which helps your tyres grip the ground. If the tread wears down, or becomes bald, this can become very dangerous as the tyres won't be able to grip the road properly and you can lose control of your car.

Most countries have laws specifying a minimum tread depth that your tyres must have. It is usually around 1.6mm.

Most new tyres have a built-in tread depth indicator. When the tyres are worn down to this level they need to be replaced.

Tread depth indicator

To get the best view for checking the tread depth indicator – turn the wheels out.

Even Wear

Under-inflated

Over-inflated

Toe-in

WHAT YOUR TYRES ARE TRYING TO TELL YOU

The way that tyres wear can tell you a great deal about your car's condition. Healthy tyres wear evenly. The tread in the middle should be slightly thicker than the edges.

Under-inflated

If the outer edges of the tyre are more worn than the centre it means your tyres tend to be under-inflated.

Over-inflated

If the tread in the centre of the tyre is more worn than the outer edges you usually drive with your tyres over-inflated.

Toe-in

If your tyres are worn more on one side than the other then you have what is known as a toe-in and you need to get your wheels re-aligned.

Tyre rotation

One way of preserving the life of your tyres is to rotate them every 5,000–7,000 miles. Ask your mechanic to do this for you while you are getting a service.

WINDSCREEN WIPERS

As you use wipers they begin to wear down. They should be changed once or twice a year, depending on their usage. Some manufacturers recommend every 6,000 to 10,000 miles.

You can tell when your wipers are wearing down as they begin to smear the glass or make a noise when they're in use.

You can purchase windscreen wipers from most petrol stations or you can go to a motor factor shop. You can also go to your car's dealer centre and purchase the manufacturer's recommended wipers – although those will probably be more expensive.

> You can replace the whole wiper blade or just replace the rubber insert, which is slightly more tricky.

1. Depending on your wiper blade you will either have to pull or push your wiper from the main body to remove it.

2.   Insert the new wiper. You will generally hear a click as it goes into place.

3. Replace the wiper to the windscreen.

WHEEL ALIGNMENT

Wheel alignment and wheel balancing are two totally different things but people often get them confused.

Wheel alignment means adjusting the angles of the wheels so they are perpendicular to the ground and parallel with each other. Aligning your wheels maximises the life of the tyres.

SIGNS YOUR WHEELS ARE OUT OF ALIGNMENT:

1. Uneven or rapid tyre wear.
2. Pulling or drifting when you are driving in a straight line.
3. The spokes of your steering wheel are off to one side when you are driving on a straight road.

If you are experiencing any of these problems you need to take your car to a mechanic or a tyre centre to get your wheels aligned.

WHEEL BALANCING

If you experience vibrations from your steering wheel, seat or floorboard when you are driving at high speeds it is likely that you need to get your wheels balanced. This is another operation that needs to be carried out by the professionals. You can take your car to your friendly local mechanic or tyre centre.

BODYWORK

Scratches and scrapes are all part of the driving process. Some people scratch and scrape more than others, but if you leave a scratch untreated rust can set in. This destroys the metal underneath and you will have to get the whole panel replaced. This is pricey!

Replacing the entire section will probably leave you out of pocket even more when you try and resell the car. Scrapes and scratches reduce the resale price of the car. Re-spraying parts can be expensive but it's worth it.

When you are having your car sprayed don't be afraid to call several places to get a quote. You may find that the quotes vary greatly and you might get yourself a great deal!

SPOTTING PROBLEMS

A FEW THINGS TO LOOK OUT FOR...

Watch out for leaks or stains under the car. If you notice your car is leaving any patches of fluid on the ground it is likely you have a leak and need to take your car to a mechanic.

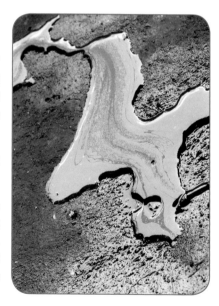

If you are constantly having to replace a fluid (e.g. oil) this means you could have a leak.

Be aware of all of your controls when you are driving and if anything feels a little unusual make a note of it and inform your mechanic. For example: stiff gear change; an unusual sensation in your pedal; your steering feels different; you hear strange noises.

WHAT IS A CAR SERVICE?

Would you get into a plane that hadn't been regularly checked by engineers to make sure everything was working properly? Didn't think so! You car is a sophisticated piece of machinery which relies on everything working as it should in order to obtain peak performance and safety. When the car manufacturers are designing and testing a car they come up with recommendations of procedures that need to be carried out in order to ensure the car they have produced works properly. Filters, fluids, belts, brake pads, spark plugs, to name a few, all need to be changed after a certain amount of time or mileage. Your car comes with a service manual which will tell the mechanic what procedures he needs to carry out depending on what mileage your car is at.

Check your **owner's manual** to find out how often you need to bring your car in for a service. Don't try and avoid it! Continually paying small amounts for ongoing service will reduce your chances of having to pay out huge whopping sums that you can't afford when major things go wrong. Think of it like investing in good skin care products – pay a little extra now and you'll avoid the hugely expensive repair work later on!

VISITING YOUR LOCAL MECHANIC

It's safe to say that most girls dread a trip to the mechanic. You nervously hand over your car, racking your brains trying to remember the last time you had it serviced. You return a few days later only to be told that this and that are wrong with it, most of which you don't understand. Then you hand over all your money and say goodbye to that two weeks in Spain with the girls. Then, there's that niggling suspicion that, could it be, Mr Local Friendly Mechanic is taking advantage of the fact that you're FEMALE?!

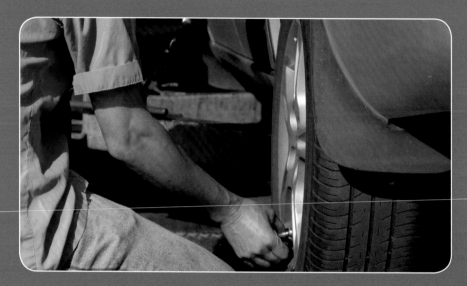

HERE ARE A FEW TIPS TO TRY AND MINIMISE THE EMOTIONAL TRAUMA:

1. Go in sounding knowledgeable. Use this book to help you determine what's wrong with your car so you can tell him what the problem is and not the other way round. If possible use some mechanical terminology to convince him.

2. Get recommendations. Ask friends to recommend a reliable and trustworthy mechanic.

3. Make sure they are qualified – don't be tempted to give your car to a mate's brother who'll do it for less.

4. If you need a lot of work done don't be afraid to haggle or call several other garages to get a comparison quote.

5. Agree the work you want the mechanic to do and ask him for an agreed price. Sometimes when they start working on the car they find other things wrong with it. Tell the mechanic to call you before he carries out any other additional work that will increase your bill when you collect your car.

6. The purpose of this book is to empower girls when it comes to their car. However, as a last resort, if you don't think you will be able to talk the talk in this situation then it might be a good idea to bring your trusty "I know all about cars" male (or female) friend with you to do the talking on your behalf. It's good to make them feel useful!

WHO DO I GO TO?

Repairing cars has become a very specialised service, so when something goes wrong with your car make sure you contact the right person.

Crash repair centres (aka panel beaters): repair any damage done to the exterior of your car.

Mechanics: carry out all work involving your engine.

Tyre centres: sell tyres and perform wheel alignment and balancing.

Auto-electricians: fix any electrical problems e.g. alarms, problems with your battery or lights.

Car dealerships: even if you didn't buy your car from an authorised dealership, occasionally when something goes wrong you will have to deal with a certified dealership for your make of car. You can find your nearest dealership by looking up your car make in the phone book. You will need to go to a dealership if you lose your car keys, have problems with your alarm or need to buy a specialised part for your car. Car dealerships can also carry out servicing, but they tend to be expensive compared to other mechanics.

CAR DOCTOR SURGERY

M.B, Ch.B., M.R.C, G.P

Section 4
CAR DOCTOR

Car Doctor...

QUESTIONS AND ANSWERS

STARTING PROBLEMS

Q. When I try to start my car, the engine won't start but there is a clicking noise. What should I do?

A. It sounds like your battery is flat. Turn to page 85 to find out how to recharge this. If your battery is more than three years old, it may be at the end of its life and so needs to be replaced.

Q. I have tried to start my car but it won't start. The headlights are working full beam though. What do you recommend?

A. It could be you have a problem with your ignition and not your battery. In this event, jump-starting may not help. You will need to call a mechanic.

PEDAL PROBLEMS

Q. When I put my foot on the brake pedal I feel a pulsating/vibrating sensation. Can you explain?

A. With ABS a pulsating effect is normal when braking hard. If you don't have an ABS system then it could mean that the brake discs are damaged. Your local mechanic should be able to replace a damaged disc for you.

Q. Sometimes when I am accelerating, there is a squealing noise. What do you think that could be?

A. It could indicate that you have a loose alternator drive belt. This can lead to other problems such as engine overheating or a flat battery so take it to your mechanic and he can tighten the belt for you.

Q. Lately when I have been pressing my foot against the brakes it feels more springy than solid. Is this something I should be worried about?

A. As brakes are a vital part of your safety system, they should not be ignored. It is more than likely that air has got into your brake system. Your brakes not only need to be bled, but your mechanic needs to determine how the air got into the system in the first place.

Q. When I try to accelerate, the revs on my rev counter increase but my car doesn't actually speed up. What is happening?

A. Your clutch has probably slipped so it needs to be overhauled by a mechanic straight away.

Q. Lately, when I put my foot on the clutch pedal, it is quite springy and when I try to put my car in first gear, I hear a grating noise. Do you know what's wrong?

A. I would say that air has got into your hydraulic system and it needs to be bled. Be wary of someone who says you need an entire (and expensive) overhaul, as this should not be the case.

EXHAUST PROBLEMS

Q. My exhaust seems to be making a lot of noise recently. What is wrong?

A. There could be a hole somewhere in your exhaust system and gases are blowing out under the car rather than out the back of it. This can be a dangerous condition so take your car to a mechanic or specialist exhaust centre.

Q. I noticed droplets of water coming from my exhaust pipe. What do you think is wrong?

A. Some condensation coming from your exhaust pipe is normal first thing in the morning as condensation has built in it overnight. However, if your engine is fully warmed up and you can still see the signs of excessive water coming from your exhaust, it could mean a more serious problem with your head gasket that will need the urgent attention of a mechanic.

Q. Sometimes when I have been sitting in traffic for a while, a cloud of blue smoke comes from my exhaust. What could that be?

A. It could be that your pistons, piston rings or valves are worn and need replacing. It is best if you take it to your mechanic to get it checked out.

ENGINE PROBLEMS

Q. I can hear a heavy knocking noise coming from my engine when I am driving. Any suggestions?

A. If the noise is coming from your engine it could be that the bearings on your engine are worn and need to be replaced. Unfortunately, this is an expensive but essential procedure.

Q. I can hear a hissing noise coming from my engine when I am driving. What is that?

A. It sounds like you have a leak in either the intake manifold or one of its associated parts. If this is the case, you will need to get your gasket tightened or replaced by a mechanic.

Q. I am driving my car normally but it feels like there is a lot less power. Can you help?

A. You probably have faulty ignition timing. You will need to take it to a mechanic to get it checked out.

Q. My engine when running vibrates violently and seriously lacks power. What do you think could be wrong?

A. It sounds like a misfire in one cylinder, possibly one ignition coil needs replacing. You will have to take it to a mechanic but luckily enough it is not a major undertaking to fix.

MISCELLANEOUS PROBLEMS

Q. I have a small crack in my windscreen. Will I need to get the whole window replaced?

A. Maybe not. There are specialist windscreen specialists who deal with these issues. You can find them in your local directory. If the hole is smaller than a £2 or €2 coin, is at least 5cm in from the edge and is not in the driver's immediate vision then they should be able to repair it without having to replace the whole windscreen. The sooner you get the crack treated the better as they can quickly increase in size.

Q. I have just put petrol into my diesel engine. What should I do?

A. If you have put less than ¼ of a tank of petrol into a diesel engine then you should be OK. Ensure you fill the rest of the tank fully with diesel. When you drive, the engine might smoke a bit but it should be fine. If there is more than ¼ of a tank of petrol in your engine then do not turn the engine on. Get it towed to a mechanic where he will need to drain the fuel tank for you.

Q. Help! I have just put diesel into my petrol engine.

A. Putting diesel into a petrol engine is much more serious than the other way around. Do not attempt to turn on the engine. The car needs to be towed to a mechanic, as he needs to drain the fuel tank and flush the system.

Q. The lights in my car are constantly blowing and needing to be replaced. Why is that?

A. It could be that your alternator voltage is set too high. This situation can be quite dangerous as the battery gives off explosive hydrogen gas if it is being overcharged so take your car to your mechanic so he can attend to it.

Q. There is a knocking noise coming from my wheels when I turn corners. What is this?

A. It sounds like the CV joints of your wheel need replacing. This can easily be carried out by your local mechanic.

Q. Recently when I have been driving over speed bumps, my car bounces a lot more than usual. What should I do?

A. I would say that you need to get new shock absorbers. A mechanic can carry this out or some tyre centres now provide this service too.

Q. While I was carrying out my maintenance checks, I noticed an excess of white powder around my battery. Is this normal?

A. This may indicate that your alternator is overcharging the battery, which can be quite dangerous. Take your car to your local mechanic so he can check the charging rate of your alternator and rectify or replace as necessary.

Section 5
CLEANING YOUR CAR

Have you ever seen a 40-year-old classic car that looked like it was just out of the car showroom or a 10-year-old car that looked faded and drab? What caused the difference? You can bet the person with the classic car was out every month cleaning and putting protective products on their car to prevent the ageing process.

Driving a nice, clean car not only makes you look and feel good, it also helps increase the resale value of the car when it is time for you to sell. Get your sponges at the ready and find out how to give your car the proper love and attention it needs to maintain its showroom look.

CLEAN AND PROTECT

Did you know that you are not only supposed to clean the surfaces of your car, but you are also meant to apply a protective covering on them?

The paint on your car is exposed to all sorts of elements – acid rain, pollution, acidic bird droppings, sap from trees – which corrode the paint, making it lose its colour and shine. Similarly, the vinyl in the interior of your car is constantly exposed to the sun's harmful UV rays and unless treated to a protection treatment every now and then the vinyl will begin to fade and look aged.

Ideally your car should get a full valet (deep clean) twice a year and then a quick clean every month – vacuum, exterior wash, wax.

GETTING SOMEONE ELSE TO DO THE DIRTY WORK

There are professional car valet companies who will do all the work for you, but it's not cheap. If you do choose to go down the car valet route, before you hand over your car don't be afraid to ask them what's involved and then when you come to collect it, make sure they have done the work they said they would do. If the price included a wax, feel the surface of your paint to make sure it was done.

The brushes in commercial car washes can be tough on your paint job. That is why some people prefer to go to "brushless" or "hand-wash" car washes which are softer on your car.

DOING IT YOURSELF

CLEANING THE EXTERIOR

First things first. Washing-up liquid has been designed with cleaning agents that remove animal fats from ceramic plates. Car shampoos have been designed to remove all the harmful substances your car's paint is likely to come into contact with, and many of them come with gloss enhancers. Which one are you going to choose to clean your car with? If you have decided to take on the task of cleaning the car yourself, take a trip to your nearest car care shop and invest in specialist good quality car cleaning products. Once you are stocked up, these products should last you several cleans.

Car cleaning - Shopping list

- Plastic bucket
- Car shampoo
- Baking soda
- Special citrus degreaser for insects and tar that just won't shift
- Proper wash mitt, pad or sponge
- Lots and lots of clean 100% cotton strips of cloth *(tear up that old T-shirt!)*
- Chamois
- Car wax
- Vacuum cleaner
- Upholstery cleaner
- Vinyl cleaner
- Small paint brush *(for getting into tricky corners)*

And if you have leather seats:

- Leather cleaner
- Leather conditioner

CAR WASH

- Read the instructions on your car shampoo to make sure you mix the right amount of mixture to water. When it comes to car shampoos, less is more, so don't overdo it.

- Clean the car in sections i.e. bonnet, boot and sides.

- Start cleaning from the top down.

- If at any time grit gets into your wash mitt or sponge, remove it immediately as it can scratch the paint.

- Be careful of bird droppings. They often contain seeds that can scratch the paint. If you come across a bird dropping, gently blot it clean with a mix of one tablespoon of baking soda in a mug of warm water.

- Try and dry the car as soon as possible after you have washed it.

- After you have rinsed the car, to dry, gently blot the water away from the surface.

- Use normal window cleaner to clean the windows.

WAX

When the car is fully dry it's time to wax!

Applying a wax to the surface of the car protects it from all the elements that try and attack it on a daily basis: acid rain, UV rays, pollution, insects, road tar.

Wax should only be applied to a clean surface.

- Wax should be applied sparingly so use your fingers or an applicator pad to apply a small amount.

- Rub the wax into the car in a linear motion, preferably in the direction air moves along your car when you are driving.

- Work the wax into the surface until all you can see is a light haze.

- When the wax has been applied, get a clean 100% cotton cloth and buff (polish).

- When you have finished the first buff go back around the car again buffing any areas where you can still see wax.

- Stand back and be proud of your lovely, shiny car.

CLEANING THE INTERIOR

- Take everything out of your car.
- Remove floor mats.
- Vacuum as many surfaces as you can.

UPHOLSTERY

- Wet a clean cloth, wring it out, and apply some upholstery cleaner.
- Clean down the upholstery with the cloth.

Be sure not to soak any of the upholstery or it won't have a chance to dry properly and will leave a mouldy smell.

CARPETS

- Bang floor mats against a surface to remove as much dirt as possible.

- Vacuum each mat on the ground.

- Spray mats evenly with carpet cleaner.

- Leave for a few minutes.

- Wipe thoroughly with a dry cloth.

- Repeat the same cleaning process for interior carpets ensuring that you don't let the carpets ever get too damp.

VINYL

Your dashboard, inside doors, steering wheel and sometimes seats and convertible tops are made from vinyl. Vinyl is sensitive to the sun's rays and can fade or become brittle over time. It is essential that you use a cleaning product that has been specially designed to clean vinyl.

- Using a dry cloth, clear away the excess dirt on all your vinyl surfaces.

- Use a small paint brush to clean the vents.

- Apply vinyl cleaners to a clean cloth and work into the surfaces.

- Go over these areas again with another clean, dry cloth.

- Apply vinyl protector.

When you have finished cleaning your car, if you can, leave the doors of the car open for 30 minutes to dry it out.

LEATHER

As leather is a natural product it isn't as enduring as man-made products so it needs a lot more love and care than upholstery seats to stay looking fresh. If you have splashed out on a car with leather seats, doesn't it make sense to look after them properly?

- Remove any excessive dirt using a vacuum cleaner.

- Use a brush to remove any dirt that may have become lodged in the grooves of the seats.

- Apply special leather cleaner and gently work into the leather.

- Clean away any excess with a clean cloth.

- Apply a leather conditioner to the seats.

Section 6
WHEN THINGS GO WRONG

WHAT TO DO IF YOU BREAK DOWN
AND YOU HAVE COVER

If your car breaks down and you feel it isn't a problem you can fix yourself, you need to pull over as soon as it is possible to do so.

- Try and park your car in the safest place possible.

- If you are on a motorway, pull it as far into the hard shoulder as possible.

- Put on your hazard lights.

- Call your breakdown assistance company.

- If you are worried that your car could be hit by oncoming traffic, when it is safe to do so get out of the car with any passengers and wait in a safe place.

- If you are able to wait in the car, lock all the doors and pull up the windows.

- If a stranger tries to talk to you, inform them that you have called for recovery and you are OK.

WHAT TO DO IF YOU BREAK DOWN AND YOU DON'T HAVE COVER

If you break down and you don't have any breakdown cover the cheapest option is to call a friend with a tow bar and a tow line, which you can purchase from most petrol stations, and ask them to tow you to a nearby garage. They might be so good as to drop you to your local one. If it is after hours, park your car somewhere safe near the garage and ask your kind friend for a lift home. Then buy them a lovely gift for being so kind.

If you don't have a friend with a tow bar then you will have to call directory enquiries and get the number of the local car recovery company in relation to where you have broken down. Be warned though, these companies can be very expensive. If you don't have the money straight away to pay them, they will take your car to a compound and charge you a fee for every day you leave it there. Then you will need to get them to take the car from the compound to a garage, which will be an additional fee.

FLAT TYRE

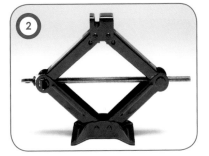

So, you are driving along, and your car begins to feel a bit bumpy and the steering starts to pull to one side – the chances are you have a flat tyre. Decide on a suitable expletive, swear loudly and pull in to the side of the road as soon as it's safe!

Changing a flat tyre seems to be the thing about cars that girls are scared of the most but it's really quite simple. You should have a **jack** in your car which does all the heavy lifting for you. The only heavy lifting you have to do is lifting the tyre itself. Believe it or not it should take you less than 15 minutes – which is quicker than waiting for someone to come and save you!

> **Warning – your hands are going to get dirty!**

WHAT YOU NEED:

1. **A safety triangle**
2. **A jack**
3. **A wheel brace**

1. Safety always comes first so make sure your hand brake is on. If you have a safety triangle place it about 10m behind the car to notify other drivers.

2. If your car has a chock – a piece of metal which you place under the front wheel to stop your car rolling – use it.

3. Prepare yourself. Set out your owner's manual, spare tyre, jack and wheel brace within the vicinity of the flat tyre. If you have a wheel cover you must lever this away from the tyre first.

4. Loosen the bolts on the tyre by revolving them about half a revolution in an anti-clockwise direction with the wheel brace. Don't be afraid to use your legs if they are very stiff! But don't remove the bolts fully yet.

Usually, you need to turn the nuts anti-clockwise to loosen and clockwise to tighten

If you have alloys you may need to remove a special bolt. Consult your **owner's manual** and follow the instructions for removing alloys.

5. Next you need to locate the "jacking point" on the car. This is a reinforced bit on the underside of your car which you place your jack under. This will take the weight of the car when the jack is raising it up without damaging the undercarriage of your car.

    You can look or feel to find the jacking point. Alternatively consult your owner's manual which should tell you where it is located.

    You need to use the jacking point which is closest to the tyre you are changing.

6. Place the jack on the ground underneath the jacking point.

7. Turn the jack in a clockwise direction.

8. Keep turning the jack until the tyre you are changing is lifted a few inches off the ground.

9. Using your fingers, the wheel brace or nut key, unscrew the nuts fully.

10. When all the nuts have been removed, lift the wheel away from the car.

11. Replace the old tyre with the spare. Warning – it can be quite tricky to align the holes in the tyres with the studs!

12. Fasten the nuts in place as tight as you can with your fingers.

13. Lower the jack. When the car has been lowered to its normal level, fully tighten the nuts with your foot until the wheel brace cannot turn any more.

Note: If you have a space saver tyre, it is only meant to be for temporary use – enough to take you to a garage or tyre centre. Do not treat this as a normal tyre.

FLAT BATTERY

Always take care when handling batteries as they contain toxic chemicals and incorrect handling can cause serious injuries. Keep children and naked flames away from the battery.

If you turn your ignition key and all you hear is a constant clicking or tapping noise it means you are having problems with your battery.

The first thing to do is to check that your battery isn't covered in dirt. If it is dirty, clean the points on the battery as this might solve the problem.

If you do this and it still doesn't work then this means your battery is dead and you will have to **jump-start** the car. But not to worry, it's really quick and easy, once you know how.

A. You will need to find a kind person who has a car with a fully charged battery and a good pair of jump leads.

B. Position the "working" car so it is front to front with the "flat" car. If it is not possible to line the cars in this way, line them up so the batteries are close together and the jump leads can reach from one battery to the other.

C. Make sure both cars are positioned in neutral.

D. Make sure the radio and the lights on the "flat" car are switched off.

Place cars bumper to bumper.

E.   Your battery may have a cover over it. If it does – remove it.

F.   Attach the red lead of the jump leads
     to the positive point on the flat car's
     battery. Usually, the positive point is
     either red in colour or has a "plus" sign
     on it.

G. Attach the other end of the red lead to
    the positive point of the working car.

H. Attach the black lead of the jump leads to the negative point on the flat car's battery. The negative point is usually black in colour and has a "minus" sign on it.

I. Attach the other end of the black lead to the negative point of the working car's battery.

J. Let the working car start up and rev its engine (in neutral) for about 20 seconds.

K. After this time turn on the ignition of the flat car and it should turn on for you.

L. If the flat car's engine begins to work, rev its engine (in neutral) and keep it running for a while to recharge the battery.

> Batteries only have a limited life span – on average 3.5 years.
> After this, once a battery starts to fail it very rarely responds to recharging and
> you will need to replace it.

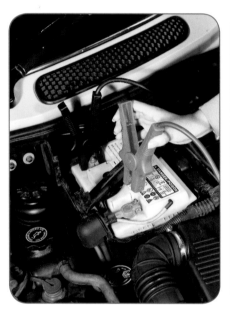

M. Now, carefully remove the jump leads from both engines.

N. It is best if you drive the formerly flat car around or leave the engine running in neutral for a while so it can recharge itself.

> Note: Just because your battery is flat doesn't necessarily mean it is
> "dead". It may just mean that you have been doing lots of short trips or have left
> it dormant and it hasn't had a chance to recharge itself.

If you're still having constant battery problems but you are sure that there is nothing wrong with your battery then you could have an alternator fault. Dim headlights can be a sign of this. Seek advice from your mechanic.

ENGINE OVERHEATING

If you are driving along and steam starts coming out of your engine and your temperature gauge reads anywhere on the "hot" level, pull over as soon as it is possible and safe to do so. Do not wait until you hit a petrol station or garage. You could cause a huge amount of expensive damage to your engine.

1. Put on your hazard lights to notify other drivers you are in trouble.

2. Open the bonnet (look under "bonnet" in your owner's manual if you don't know how to do this).

3. Do not touch any part of the engine as it will be extremely hot and could burn you.

4. Your engine can take a long while to cool down to a level that is safe to touch so be patient.

5. Turn on the heating in the car full blast. This takes the heat away from the engine.

6. You will need to add coolant but you can use water in an emergency situation. Either of these will need to be lukewarm as putting cold water in a hot engine can cause it to crack. You may need to source these while you are waiting for the engine to cool down.

7. If you hover your hand above the radiator you should be able to tell when it is cool enough to touch. Even then you might want to cover your hand with a rag or material while you are opening it. It is likely that steam will gush out of the radiator and you do not want to get scalded.

 8. At arm's length, slowly add the lukewarm coolant or water to the **radiator cap** (see **owner's manual** for location if you are unsure).

9. Only drive the car if the temperature gauge returns to normal.

10. You need to take your car to a mechanic ASAP so do not plan to drive long distances.

11. If your car begins to overheat again pull over and call your local recovery company. Your car is likely to have serious problems and driving it any further can cause terminal damage.

LOST KEYS

If you lose your keys and your car was made before the year 2000 you might be in luck. If you can find out the vehicle identification number of your car (consult your **owner's manual** to find it), then call a locksmith or your local dealer as they should be able to cut a new key for you.

However, if your car was made after the year 2000 it is more than likely that losing your key is going to turn into an expensive and troublesome experience! Most car keys made after 2000 have a special microchip, called a **transponder**, in the body of the key.

When you put your key into the ignition there is a device which reads the microchip and will only allow the key to turn if it has this special microchip in it. So, if you lose your keys you are going to have to get a new key with a microchip. Locksmiths do not have the capability to programme these microchips, so you must get it programmed at a car dealership.

WHAT TO DO NEXT:

1. Unless your local dealership has a service where they can come to you, you will have to get your car towed to your nearest car dealership – expense number one.

2. They will cut the key for you – expense number two.

3. Then they will programme the key for you – expense number three.

4. Note that car dealerships are only open during normal working hours so if you lose your keys outside of these hours, there is nothing you can do until they re-open.

> Now that you can appreciate how troublesome and expensive losing a key is, try to make sure you keep your spare set of keys somewhere safe. Replacing a lost key nowadays will dig into your holiday fund!

FAULTY ALARM

Occasionally, it can happen that your alarm will go off for no reason. This suggests that you have a fault in your alarm system. It will siren for four or five hours before it flattens the battery and dies. By then you'll have a grumpy neighbour AND a flat car battery to add to your woes!

It is unlikely your mechanic will be able to solve the problem. If your alarm is faulty you will have to get this repaired by an auto-electrician or your car dealership.

WHAT TO DO AFTER A CAR ACCIDENT

Being involved in a car accident, no matter how small, can be quite an upsetting experience so the most important thing is to stay calm. Even if there is only a small amount of damage done to either of the cars, the cost of repairing this could be surprisingly expensive. The person at fault is the person responsible for paying any damages. They won't have to pay for it personally. This is why you pay for insurance.

In order for both parties' insurance companies to be able to handle the situation correctly you need to carry out certain steps. If you don't carry out these procedures then you risk ending up having to pay for the repairs yourself. Even if it wasn't your fault.

If you have been involved in a car crash **DO NOT** admit any liability (that it was your fault). Even if you were in the wrong. When you are dealing with the other driver(s), deal with the situation as factually as possible and try to make an accurate record of what happened. You can deal with a situation factually without apportioning any blame to anyone. Leave it up to your insurance company to decide.

ACCIDENT PROTOCOL

1. Stay calm. Just take lots of deep breaths and try and calm your mind.

2. When it is safe to do so, get out of the car and assess the situation.

3. Determine whether or not you need to call the police.

You *don't* need to call the police if:

- the car(s) have only suffered minor material damage and are still roadworthy. You do not have to call the police but you can call them if you want to.

You *do* need to call the police if:

- anybody complains of physical injury.

- there is a significant amount of damage to either of the cars and they are unroadworthy.

- the crash is a result of an illegal driving manoeuvre, such as somebody jumping a red light.

If you call the police they should oversee the situation for you but for your own peace of mind it would be worthwhile to ensure that all of the following points have been carried out.

HOW TO HANDLE A MINOR CAR CRASH WITHOUT THE POLICE

If you both feel there is no need to call the police then you will need to do the following:

1. Quickly try and take a few pictures of the crash scene at different angles before moving the cars. If you don't have a camera, is there a camera on your phone? If neither party has a camera phone ask a passerby. If you still can't source a camera then take the time to sketch out the scene so you have a record of it.

2. When you have taken a record of the scene, move the cars out of the way of the moving traffic.

3. Get a pen and paper. If neither of you have one, perhaps save the details in your phone? You need to get the following information from the other party and similarly you must give all your details to them.

---

1. *Name*
2. *Address*
3. *Telephone number*
4. *Insurance company they are with & policy number (you can find both these pieces of information from the insurance disc on their windscreen)*
5. *If they are not the owner of the car (e.g. company vehicle, hire car) then you need to get the name and contact details of the organisation that owns the car*
6. *The car's registration number*
7. *Description of car (colour and make)*
8. *Date, time and location of accident*
9. *Names and contact details of any witnesses who saw the accident*

---

4. At your earliest convenience (preferably within 24 hours) go to a police station and report the accident. You need to do this for insurance purposes.

5. Contact your insurance company and tell them what happened.

Section 7
BUYING A CAR

We girls can be a bit impulsive

when it comes to buying things. We see something we really like and we want it NOW without stepping back, taking a breath and making sure we can actually afford it. You only need to look at your last credit card statement to realise that! But buying a car is a big commitment and one that you need to take some time making a decision on. If this is your first time buying a car and you just love the new Mini Cooper you might be a bit disappointed when you investigate things further and find out that you can't actually afford it. It is not just the cost of buying the car itself that comes into account. There are lots of other very significant extra costs that come with owning and running a car. Before you even begin to start looking at cars, the first thing you need to do is figure out how much you have to spend.

FIGURING OUT WHAT YOU CAN *REALLY* AFFORD

The best thing to do is look at your monthly income and see how much you can afford to set aside for the luxury (yes, it is a luxury) of owning a car. Once you have determined how much you have to spend, read through the next few points to become aware of the real cost of owning and running a car so you can choose the car that won't leave you financially crippled!

THE CAR ITSELF

So you see a car you really like. How much are they selling it for? Usually banks give car loans for a 60-month period so divide the cost of the car by 60. This is how much roughly your monthly repayments will be. In reality they will be slightly higher as you will have interest to pay on top of that, but at least it is a ballpark figure you can work from. Can you afford to pay that amount each month? If this is the first car you are going to buy and this figure is stretching you – don't even think about it. This is only one cost of motoring. If you already own a car, have you taken all the other costs of motoring – which you are perhaps used to spending – into account yet?

THE OTHER COSTS OF MOTORING

PETROL

Determine:

- How many kilometres are you planning on doing each month?

- How many kilometres does your car do to a litre?

- How much is the price of petrol per litre?

Use the calculation below to estimate your monthly petrol cost.

$$\frac{\text{Kilometres per month}}{\text{Kilometres per litre}} \times \text{ price of petrol per litre} = \text{monthly petrol cost}$$

CAR TAX

Look up the government motor tax websites to find out how much the tax on the car you are interested in will cost each year and divide that by 12 to get a monthly figure.

INSURANCE

Call up the insurance companies and get a quote on your insurance for the car. They will often give you an annual and a monthly quote.

MAINTENANCE

Ideally you should get your car serviced twice a year. Call up your local mechanic and ask him to estimate how much he thinks a service on the car you are interested in might cost.

UNEXPECTED COSTS

Unfortunately when you own a car you encounter some unexpected expenses. Trips to the mechanic and body shop are never cheap and you never know when something is going to crop up. Just be aware that you will more than likely have to shell out several hundred pounds every year on unexpected expenses.

Now that you have all your figures at the ready, calculate the total monthly cost of owning that car.

MONTHLY COST OF RUNNING A CAR

1) Monthly Repayments	
2) Petrol	
3) Insurance	
4) Car Tax	
5) Maintenance	
6) Unexpected Costs	
TOTAL MONTHLY COST	

If the cost is much more than you can afford try looking for an older but cheaper car, or a car with a smaller sized engine which will lower your petrol, insurance and tax costs.

BUYING NEW, USED OR LEASING

Now that you have decided how much you can afford to spend on the car, you need to decide which finance option best suits your needs: buying new, used or leasing.

You are about to part with a significant amount of the money you worked hard to earn so you want to make sure you make the right and informed decision and buy a car that suits your personal and financial needs. You also need to ensure that you will get some money back on it when you go on to sell it some time in the future.

But which option is best for you? Outlined here are the pros and cons of each of the different types of strategies.

BUYING A NEW CAR

THE ADVANTAGES

Some people just love the feel of owning a new car: the smell, the pristine condition, having the latest registration plates.

One of the biggest advantages of buying new is that you get the manufacturer's warranty. A warranty is a guarantee from the manufacturer of that car that the car will perform the way they say it will. Warranties are usually given for a set amount of years (usually three) or a set amount of miles (say 36,000) or whichever comes first.

This means that if you have any component problems with the car during this period, you just bring it back to the dealer; they will repair it and you shouldn't have to pay anything.

THE DISADVANTAGES

But this all comes with a price. The single biggest disadvantage to buying a new car is depreciation.

Depreciation is the decline in value of your car over the course of its life. Say the lifespan of your car is 15 years. Every year your car becomes worth a little less until 15 years later it is completely worthless and is only fit for the scrap heap. However, the rate at which your car devalues each year isn't even. It doesn't devalue by the same amount every year. It tends to rapidly decrease in value in the first three years and then stabilise after that.

Typically they say that a car loses 30% of its value as soon as it is driven out of the car showroom. So, if you just paid £20,000 for a brand new car, a week later it is now only worth £14,000 (70% of the original cost). This can be a great argument for buying a "nearly new" car. Some cars can lose up to 50% of their value in the first year!

However, it should be noted that not all cars depreciate at the same rate. Some cars hold their value better than others. So if you have your heart set on buying a new car then it would be worth your while investigating how the car you are looking at is likely to depreciate.

WHY DO CARS DEPRECIATE AT DIFFERENT RATES?

Think of it like buying a rare, coveted designer handbag that there is a waiting list for. You may have to spend a fortune on it but you can use it for a year and then if you tire of it you can sell it and you will still have lots of interested parties who are willing to pay you good money for it.

However, if you buy a not-so-expensive handbag by one of the mass-produced high street brands, and after a year you want to try and sell it on eBay, even if it is mint condition you aren't going to get a good price because there are loads of the same bag already for sale!

It's the same with cars. If you buy a mass-produced car from one of the well-known car manufacturers, when the time comes to sell your car there are more than likely going to be lots of other people selling the same car at the same time as you. Alternatively, if you have a rare or limited edition car, when it comes to selling it you could have lots of interested parties all outbidding each other to buy your car, therefore bumping up the price.

HOW CAN I FIGURE OUT HOW MUCH MY CAR IS GOING TO DEPRECIATE?

The best trick is to go online and see how much one-year-old versions of your car are selling for. If you are looking at buying a new Renault Clio, go online and look at what a one-year-old similar Renault Clio is selling for. Take this away from the price you are about to pay for yours and it will give you an indication of how much your car will devalue in the first year. If you are planning on holding on to it for three years, check what a three-year-old model is selling for. Remember, sometimes it loses most of its value in the first year and then the drop in price can tail off.

Still got your heart set on buying new? If you have factored in depreciation and are still happy to go ahead, then at least you won't get a shock when you go on to sell it and find out that you can only get a lot less than you originally paid.

LEASING

WHAT IS LEASING?

Leasing is when you rent/hire a car for a specified amount of time with an agreed preset amount of miles from a car leasing company at a fixed monthly rate.

At the end of the lease contract you give back the car to the car leasing company, pay any additional costs you may have incurred, e.g. by going over the agreed miles, or if you caused any excessive wear and tear and that's it!

The difference between leasing and buying a car is like renting or buying an apartment. If you rent an apartment it is not as big a commitment as buying, but when you have finished with it, you have nothing to show for it.

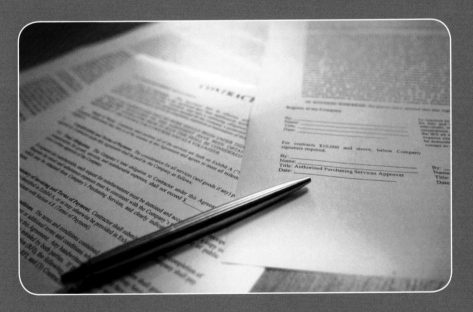

THE ADVANTAGES OF LEASING:

1. You can drive a newer, more prestigious car for your budget than if you were to buy a car outright.

2. Your monthly repayments will be lower than if you bought a car.

3. As only newer models are let out to lease, they tend to still be under the manufacturer's warranty so you should have less expensive maintenance costs.

4. The up-front costs you have to pay will be lower than the amount you would have to find if you were buying a car.

5. You can ask for the option to purchase the car at the end of the lease agreement if you feel you might decide you want to keep it. If this is something you feel you might be interested in, agree the price before you sign the lease.

6. At the end of the lease agreement you don't have to worry about the hassle of selling the car.

THE DISADVANTAGES:

1. You have to sign up for a set amount of time. If, for some reason, you need to get rid of the car, for example because you have to move, are going travelling, changing jobs, etc., you are bound to the contract, which can be very expensive to get out of.

2. You are set to a strict amount of miles you can do every year (typically 15,000 miles); if you go over this amount of miles you have to pay for each additional mile you drive and this can be pricey.

3. Alternatively, if you only drive a fraction of the agreed mileage then you are paying for miles which you never used.

4. When you are finished with the car you have nothing to show for it. You have no car equity.

5. You don't actually own the vehicle so can't make any modifications to it.

6. You have to keep the car in good condition. There is obviously some unavoidable wear and tear that comes with driving so a lease contract will typically have a "wear and tear" agreement, but if you are a fender-bender driver or have kids or pets which you take with you, you might cause more damage than is expected and you will have to pay for this at the end.

THE IDEAL CANDIDATE

- You drive around 15,000 miles a year.

- You keep your car in good condition.

- There are no future circumstances, that you are aware of anyway, which will force you to sell your car in the next three years.

If you decide that leasing is for you, the most important thing is to make sure you trust the company you are dealing with. Read the agreement very carefully and make sure you are happy with all the clauses. If you are unsure of what something means, don't be afraid to ask. Remember the person you are dealing with is a sales rep on commission. No matter how aloof they may appear to be, they want to get your business so don't be afraid to haggle or get them to change parts of the agreement which aren't suited to you.

BUYING A USED CAR

ADVANTAGES

The main advantage of buying a used car is that you can get great value for money. £10,000 might buy you a new economy-sized car or a five-year-old sporty little number.

If it is up to three years old the car could still be under its manufacturer's warranty which you can still avail yourself of should you have any problems.

While there is a risk involved in buying a new car (see the disadvantages section) there are now lots of Car History Check companies out there who can help minimise the risk.

DISADVANTAGES

The main disadvantage when you are buying a used car is the risk involved. There are lots of things that can happen to a car during its lifetime which can greatly devalue a car (such as it was involved in a big crash, or has had lots of engine trouble) which the person selling to you might not disclose properly so they can get as much money from you as possible. Also, legally there is very little comeback when buying a second-hand car, particularly in a private sale.

But have no fear, there are ways to minimise the risk. Yes, there is slightly more hassle involved but if you know what you are doing you can get a great deal.

TRICKS THE BAD GUYS PLAY AND HOW TO SPOT THEM

Unfortunately there are some bad guys out there who make a lot of money by obtaining cars with a shady background and selling them on for a lot more money than they are worth. You could potentially fork out all your money only to find out shortly afterwards that all is not what it seems, and you may even have to hand the car over to the police or previous owners (in the case that it was stolen) and you will not get one penny back. You may as well have taken your money and flushed it down the toilet. So, outlined below are the tricks people try and play, but fortunately there are ways to spot them!

UNPAID FINANCE

Outstanding unpaid finance on a car is one of the most common problems that happens today. If someone buys a car with a loan, technically the car is the property of the bank or institution they borrowed the money from until all the monies have been paid. However, some people try and sell their car while they still have an outstanding loan on it. If you buy a car that has an outstanding loan on it when you go to get insurance etc. the banks will track that a car they still technically own is being sold off and they have every right to repossess the car from you. The best way to avoid this, and most of the common problems, is to get a history check on the car. Go to the end of this section for more details.

CLOCKED

If a car has been "clocked" this means that someone has tampered with the odometer – the device on the dashboard that says how many miles the car has done in total. They usually reduce the figure to make it appear the car has done fewer miles than it actually has so you will pay more for it.

Again, a history check can sometimes pick up if a car has been clocked. Alternatively, a good idea is to look at the service manual. If the last service stamp says it was carried out at 60,000 miles and the odometer reads 40,000 you know it has been clocked!

WRITTEN OFF

If a car has been involved in a serious accident an insurance company can sometimes declare that the car is too dangerous to be put back on the road and it is "written off". Unfortunately some shady mechanics can fix up these cars so that they look OK and then go on to sell them. Your history check should tell you if it has ever been written off.

STOLEN

Thousands of cars get stolen every year with the objective of being sold on again for money. If you buy a stolen car, when you go to do things like pay for the tax and insurance you have to give your registration number and these companies have databases of stolen registration plates so alarm bells will start ringing. You will get a nice friendly visit from a police officer who will take the car from you and no matter how innocent you were of the fact it was stolen, you won't see a penny.

CLONED

Car thieves can be clever little chaps and are becoming very good at disguising the fact that a car was stolen. One such trick is "cloning". Cars are usually identified by their make, model and registration plates. If they steal, say, a red 2003 Honda Civic they will look for a similar red 2003 Civic on the road and take down their registration plate details, get a copy made, take off the registration plates from the stolen car and put the copied plates on it. Now, there are two very similar cars driving around. It is more than likely that one person has no idea their car has been cloned. The cloned car can pick up speeding tickets, parking fines, or worse, be involved in a hit and run or robbery but they will all be traced back to the innocent person's home address!

RINGING

"Ringing" is another trick to disguise a stolen car. Thieves steal a car and find a similar car that was written off, steal their registration plates and put them on the stolen car.

CUT 'N' SHUT

Say a 2004 type Opel Tigra was involved in a crash and the front has been completely destroyed. They find another 2004 Opel Tigra that was involved in a crash and the back was completely destroyed. They weld together the "good" parts of both the vehicles to make one car.

A good welder can do a superb job of hiding the seams but if you buy the car and are involved in an accident the joins can be very weak and will crumple under the pressure of a crash. Again, a history check should determine this for you.

HOW CAN I PREVENT THIS?

While the registration plates can be easily changed, the Vehicle Identification Number (VIN) cannot. All cars have to be assigned a unique VIN number when they are manufactured in the factory. They are typically made up of numbers and letters and are 17 digits long.

WHERE CAN I FIND MY VIN?

Look up "Vehicle Identification Number" or "Chassis Number" in the owner's manual of the car you are interested in. That should tell you where it is located. The VIN can be put in different places on different cars but here are a few common places to look. When you have found the VIN, give this to the History Check Company and they will be able to tell if it has been stolen.

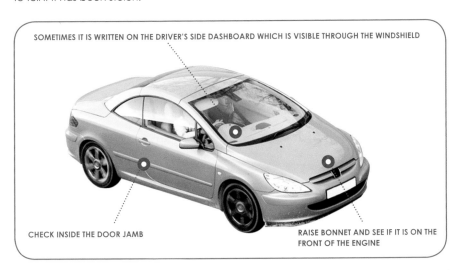

SOMETIMES IT IS WRITTEN ON THE DRIVER'S SIDE DASHBOARD WHICH IS VISIBLE THROUGH THE WINDSHIELD

CHECK INSIDE THE DOOR JAMB

RAISE BONNET AND SEE IF IT IS ON THE FRONT OF THE ENGINE

HISTORY CHECK

The best way to ensure your car hasn't got a shady past is to get a history check. These are relatively inexpensive but worth their weight in gold. Before you even go to the effort of checking the car, ask the seller for the registration number and VIN of the car and get it checked out.

Companies that carry out such checks include:

UK
www.rac.co.uk
www.hpi.co.uk

Ireland
www.motorcheck.ie
www.cartell.ie
www.carsireland.ie

GOING TO LOOK AT A SECOND-HAND CAR

OK. So, you've found the car of your dreams, you have done the maths and figured out that you will be able to afford it. Now you have to go and look at it; but what exactly should you look at? Ideally you want a car that has been well maintained and doesn't appear to have that much wrong with it. What you don't want is to buy a used car with loads of problems that ends up becoming a money pit for you. Going to have a proper look at the car is essential to make sure you don't have any major problems after you have bought it.

Here is a list of all the checks you need to carry out. None of the checks are hard; it just might take you a while to carry them all out. But you are about to spend a lot of money, so you want to make sure you are making the right decision.

Don't assume that if you bring a bloke with you he will know what he is doing. Bring this book with you and run through it as you go along if need be.

BEFORE YOU BEGIN...

1. Arrange to look at it in the morning so that the car has been parked in the same place overnight and you will be able to see if the car has left any leaks.

2. When you first meet the seller ask them to give you a history of the car: has it been involved in any accidents? Have there been any major problems with the engine? They may disclose these things to you and be offering you the car at a reduced price. But if they don't tell you and you find things wrong then they are hiding stuff from you and alarm bells should start ringing.

3. Ask them for a copy of the service history manual and the owner's manual. Look at the service history. It should be dated and stamped by every mechanic who did work on it. A car should be serviced every six months to keep it in top order. Have they been doing it? Does the service manual say that they got any major work done which they didn't tell you about? They may say that they have lost the book. It does happen; if so, ask them for the name of their mechanic, call him up and ask him directly how often he tended to it and what he did.

4. Look up "timing belt" in the **owner's manual**. It should say when it needs to be changed. How many miles has your car done? Is it past or is it coming close to the time when the timing belt needs to be changed? If so, ask the person about it. They got it changed? If so – ask for proof. If not, this is something that you will have to pay for soon. Just be aware that it is going to be an added expense in the near future.

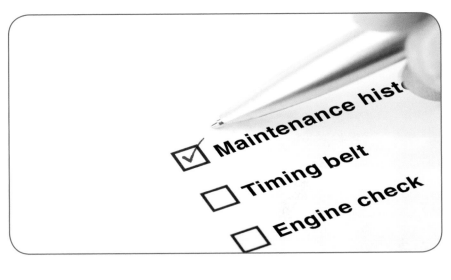

UNDER THE BONNET

- Open the bonnet. Ask them to do it for you or else look under "bonnet" in the owner's manual and it will tell you how to open it.

- Check the oil, coolant and brake fluid to make sure they are all OK. Refer to the car maintenance section on how to do this.

- Now have a look at the engine and inspect any belts or hoses you can see. Do they look cracked or worn?

- Look around the radiator. If there are white stains around it, it could be a sign that the engine has overheated at some stage.

- Have a look at the battery and make sure it looks clean enough. Ask them the last time they got it changed. Batteries need to be changed roughly every three years. If it has been a while since they got it changed, you will have to fork out for a new one.

WALKING AROUND THE CAR

Now that you have the engine checked out, you need to look at the external things.

Under the car
Get down on your knees and look under the car. Can you see any patches that could indicate a leak?

Tyres
Have a careful look at the tyres to make sure they are all in good condition. Make sure there are no cracks, excessive wearing or bumps. Make sure the tread depth is OK on them and they are not bald. Check them all and don't forget the spare. If they look old and worn remember it is illegal to drive with poor tyres so you will have to pay for new ones.

Suspension
Walk around to each corner of the car and give it a good push down. The car should bounce back once or twice and then stop. This is a good indication the suspension is OK.

Body of the car
Walk around the car and carefully look at the bodywork. Look out for any noticeable scrapes, dents or rust. Check all the seams too (where two pieces of metal meet, i.e. the door frames or bonnet) and look for any signs that this section of the car has been resprayed. This could be an indication it has been involved in an accident.

INTERIOR

Now open all the doors, including the boot, and have a look at the upholstery, carpet and vinyl and make sure you are happy with the appearance of them. As these features don't actually affect the driving ability and safety of the car you can still drive it. But if they are excessively worn you can use this as a good bargaining tool for reducing the price.

BEHIND THE DRIVER'S SEAT

Leaving the car in neutral turn on the engine.

- Open and close all the windows.

- Turn on the radio to make sure it is working.

- If the car has air conditioning, test it.

- Turn on the wipers.

- Test the locks.

- Now, turn on all the lights, including the hazard lights, get out of the car, walk around all four corners and make sure they are all working.

THE TEST DRIVE

Now that you have checked that you are happy with everything, you will need to take the car for a test drive. If you already own a car, make sure you are covered in your own insurance policy to drive someone else's car.

If you are a first-time driver and don't have insurance yet you will need to get someone else who is covered to drive it for you. Sit in the front seat with them and make sure they carry out the following checks.

THE ENGINE

As you are driving, turn off the radio and air conditioning, open the windows and listen to the sound of the engine. It should be smooth and not making too much noise. Then turn your head towards the back of the car and try and listen to the exhaust. It should be reasonably quiet also.

SUSPENSION

If you can, try and get the car driven over some speed bumps and make sure you are happy with the suspension.

THE BRAKES

Test the brakes in normal traffic and against traffic lights. Make sure they work efficiently; there should be no noises coming from them.

When it is safe to do so, try and get the car to stop suddenly. How did the brakes react?

Test the hand brake and make sure it pulls up easily.

THE GEARS

The gear change should be smooth and easy. If it is very difficult to change gears then it could mean that the gearbox is nearing the end of its life. You will have to replace it sometime in the near future and this is very expensive.

WHEEL ALIGNMENT

When you are driving on a straight stretch of road, really loosen your grip on the steering wheel. The car should continue to drive straight for you. If it veers off to one side this means the wheel alignment is off. This can be easily fixed – but for a charge of course.

CONVERTIBLE

If you are buying a convertible, make sure you test the hood – go through the whole process – and make sure there are no problems.

PROFESSIONAL CHECK

So, if you are happy that there is nothing majorly wrong with the car you can still get a mechanic to check the car properly for you. You are going to have to pay him for this but it might be worth it for peace of mind.

HOW MUCH SHOULD I PAY FOR IT?

You have found the car of your dreams, done a history check, inspected it yourself and are happy with it. How much should you actually be paying for it?

Go online and look at **www.whatcar.com** for a guide price. If you have got a mechanic to check it out why not ask him how much he thinks it is worth? If you haven't gone down the mechanic route look online and see how much similar cars in age and mileage are selling for. This will give you a starting point but you should be able to haggle down the price if any of the following things are wrong.

- Your car has excessive mileage compared to other cars on sale which are the same year.

- There are scrapes and scratches on the body. These ultimately won't affect the driving ability or safety of the car so it is a personal choice if you don't mind driving with them but you should definitely be looking for a few hundred off the asking price if they are there.

- The interior hasn't been well maintained.

If there are problems which can be fixed – such as the car needs new tyres or wheel alignment – you can take away the cost of repairing these from the quote but remember you will end up with the hassle and expense of doing it yourself.

THE PAPERWORK

Once you have handed over all monies for the car, you need to fill in your details on the Vehicle Registration Certificate and the former owner needs to sign it. The Certificate then needs to be posted to the DVLA (UK) or Department of Environment (Ireland) in order for the car to be legally registered as being yours.

Also ensure you get the owner's manual, service log book and spare keys from the existing owners and that's it! Congratulations on getting a new car!

Section 8
SELLING A CAR

When it comes to selling a car,

you have three options.

1. Sell it to a car dealer.

2. Get the price of the car offset against buying a new car from a dealer – known as a "trade in".

3. Sell the car privately yourself.

If you sell your car to a dealer, you can avoid all the hassle of selling a car but as the dealer still needs to sell it on and make a profit, you will get the lowest price possible for the car.

If your car is in bad condition though, sometimes the dealers can offer the best price as they have the ways and means of fixing your car cheaply.

HOW MUCH IS IT WORTH?

The quickest way to find out how much your car is worth is to go online.

Websites such as **www.parkers.com** and **www.glass.co.uk** offer a valuation service based on your make, model, year, mileage and condition. There is however a small fee for the service.

You can actually figure out this information for free. Go onto websites that sell cars, such as **www.autotrader.co.uk** and look at how the exact same make, model and year of your car with similar mileage is selling for. Write down three or four prices and calculate an average based on these prices.

> If going online just isn't for you then you can purchase a car selling magazine to get the average price.

This price will give you a starting figure to work from. If your car has lots of extra features, or is a special edition, then you can look to sell it for the price of a car that is a year younger than yours.

WHAT CONDITION IS YOUR CAR IN?

Next, you need to determine what condition your car is in. Have a good look at your car and determine the following:

	Excellent	Expected for age	Poor
Engine:			
Have you been having any problems with your engine lately? Have you been good at taking your car for regular services and keeping a record in your maintenance logbook?			
Paintwork:			
Are there any scratches or dings on your paintwork or is it as good as new?			
Tyres:			
How deep is the tread in your tyres? Are there any cracks or bulges?			
Interior:			
What is the condition of your upholstery, carpets and vinyl? Don't forget to look at the boot.			
Electrics:			
Are your radio, electric windows, lights, air conditioning (if you have it) working OK?			

If your car is in excellent condition, you can expect to charge the top price for it. If it is in poor condition, you can expect the buyer to try to haggle down the asking price.

Once you have determined your price, you should add on a few extra hundred pounds as most people will expect you to negotiate on price. This will give you some extra leeway. Don't however put the price up too high as this will scare people off. If you are looking at prices online you can expect that they have also included "negotiation" leverage so perhaps follow their lead, but expect to sell it for a few hundred less.

SHOULD I FIX IT?

If you have something wrong with your car such as engine trouble or it needs bodywork done, you will have to decide whether you want to pay for it to be fixed or whether you would prefer to take the cost of the repairs from the asking price and get the new owner to pay for it. If you don't have the money to pay for the work yourself you would be surprised at how many people out there would take a car that needs work done to it for a reduced price. Just be sure to include the information on the ad.

PUTTING THE CAR UP FOR SALE

Currently, the most common place for people to look to buy a car is online. There are lots of websites such as **www.autotrader.co.uk** where you can place your ad, and there are also car magazines which you can contact. If the internet just isn't for you, then placing an ad in your local newspaper still works!

THE AD

Ads with pictures make quicker sales so go out and clean the car, park it in a nice place and take some good pictures of it.

Include the make, model, year, engine size, mileage and colour, as well as fuel type (petrol or diesel) and transmission (manual or automatic).

Bring out the saleswoman in you and put down any special features your car has – but be honest.

Which of the following are true for your car? If you have them – put them in!

- MOT/NCT
- Excellent condition
- Good condition
- Low mileage
- Full service history
- Power steering
- New tyres
- Electric windows
- Air conditioning
- Sunroof
- Convertible
- Colour-coded bumpers (when the bumpers are the same colour as the rest of the car)
- Airbags
- Alloy wheels
- CD player
- Any other custom modifications

VIEWING THE CAR

If someone is interested in buying your car, they will want to come and inspect it. For safety reasons it is better that they come to your house. Have someone there with you if you are worried about your personal safety. First impression is everything so make sure you freshly clean the car before they come. Have your owner's manual and maintenance log at the ready.

TEST DRIVE

The buyer will more than likely want to take the car for a test drive. You are not obliged to allow them to take one, but it will probably increase the chances of sale if you do. Make sure that your car is insured to allow someone else to drive your car or the buyer is covered under their own policy. Unless you want someone to drive off with a free car always go on the test drive with them. Don't forget to fully lock your house before you leave.

NEGOTIATING THE PRICE

Know in your mind exactly what the minimum price you would be willing to sell your car for is. Do not tell them what your lowest price is and do not go below it. If you have had several callers this means you shouldn't need to haggle down on price. Some people are great at haggling. They will try to make you feel that your car is worthless and you would be lucky to get their custom at a greatly reduced price but don't fall for their tricks. If they are offering less than you feel is right, based on your research of the market, just say no. You might be surprised that they will suddenly pay your asking price. There is an art to haggling!

THE MONEY BIT

The cardinal rule you need to remember here is do not hand over the car to anyone until the money is sitting safely in your bank account. Cheques can bounce and banker's drafts can be forged so make sure that the money actually goes through before you release your car.

As cars are an expensive commodity, buyers rarely have enough cash to hand to pay the full amount immediately. It is more than likely that they will want to put a deposit on the car until they arrange financing. If someone is interested, make sure you get a non-refundable deposit for a set amount of time. You do not want to be waiting around for a month to accept payment.

In the interest of both parties it is important that you draft a proper receipt. Ensure that you make two copies – one for you, one for them. Here is a sample of what you need to include.

Seller's details	Buyer's details
Name:	Name:
Address:	Address:
Contact:	Contact:
Price agreed:	Price agreed:
Deposit amount:	Deposit amount:
Final date full monies due:	Final date full monies due:
Signature:	Signature:
Date:	Date:

SAYING FAREWELL

Once all monies have been paid and both parties are satisfied with the deal then you will need to hand over all your car documentation and spare keys to the new owner. The new owner needs to fill in their details on the car's registration documents and you will need to sign the bottom of it. This should be posted to:

- DVLA (UK)
- Department of Environment (Ireland)

Section 9
YOUR CAR AND
THE ENVIRONMENT

OK girls, let's face it, we love our cars but we also love our home, planet Earth! You would have to be living under a rock not to know that the CO_2 emissions from cars are contributing to global warming. If you want to know how you can help here are some handy tips.

HOW CAN I HELP?

Choose a car with the lowest CO$_2$

Environmentally conscious people can compare cars by the grammes of CO$_2$ they produce per kilometre. The lower the grammes of CO$_2$ emissions the better. Check out a website such as **www.carpages.co.uk/co2/** to find out how your car compares. Fuel efficient cars are cheaper to run so will be kinder on your pocket too. If you fancy choosing a car with an alternative fuel, turn to page 32 to find out more.

Go neutral

If you feel like being really good you can offset your annual carbon emissions. You might be surprised at how inexpensive it is. Carbon offset companies calculate how many tonnes of CO$_2$ your car has added to the atmosphere and then they offset these emissions with ventures, such as planting trees, to soak up the carbon you personally produced. Go online to companies such as **www.carbonfund.org** and get planting.

Do you really need to use your car this time?

It can be hard to function in today's society without a car but a lot of us can get into the habit of becoming too dependent on our cars and you might have noticed your waistline expanding too! Try to cut out using your car for any trips under a mile. Walk or cycle instead. If there is a public transport system that can get you to your destination, why don't you leave the car at home and use that instead? Let someone else negotiate the traffic and parking for you!

Car pool

Is there someone you can share a lift to work with? Car pooling is a great way of reducing the amount of cars unnecessarily on the road and a great way of catching up on the gossip too!

Keep your car tuned

If you keep your car tuned by carrying out the regular maintenance checks in this book and by ensuring your car is regularly serviced, it will run at its optimum level and live for longer. Cars that are not running at their optimum become inefficient and unnecessarily use petrol.

Pump up the pressure

If your tyres are under-inflated, your engine has to work much harder to get your car to move. By regularly checking your tyre pressure you will not only save about 10% on your annual fuel bill, you will also extend the life of your tyres and reduce the amount of wasted tyres that are produced unnecessarily every year.

Buying second hand

If you buy a second-hand car you save all the energy and resources it takes to create a new car.

Saving water

The average person washing their car with a hose uses 180 litres of water, whereas if you use a bucket you only use about 10 litres.

Get rid of the junk in your trunk

The heavier your car is, the more petrol it needs to move. Get rid of any unnecessary heavy items that you might be carrying in your boot. If you have a roof rack and you are not using it, take it down.

Be friendly to the fish

If even the tiniest bit of oil gets into a fresh water system it chokes the poor little fish. When you are having your car serviced ask your mechanic to ensure that any unused car parts and oil are properly disposed of. There are professional companies who will do this for your mechanic. If he is not using this facility as standard, you can request that he does use such a company. He might request you contribute towards the cost but by now we should know that we all have to take responsibility for the waste we produce.

Keeping things streamlined

If you are driving at top speed and have the window or sunroof open, you are creating a lot of drag and your car will need to burn more fuel to go at the same speed compared to if the windows were closed. More fuel means more money, which is never cool.

Staying cool

The air-conditioning system in a car uses up a lot of energy and most people use it unnecessarily. The vents in your car are designed to bring cool air in for free! When you are sitting in traffic why not open the window to cool down?

INDEX

A

ABS	30,38
accelerator	7,59
accident	95-97
air filter	14-15
alloy wheels	19
alternator	38,59,63,90
alternator belt	14, 59
anti-freeze	42
auto-electrician	55,94
automatic	31
axles	9

B

battery	38,55,58,63,85–90
bearings	5,10,61
belts	14
biodiesel	32
bodywork	55
bonnet	39
brake fluid	43
brake fluid reservoir	43
brake horsepower	26
brake pads	16
brakes	16,30,38,59,124
breakdown - with cover	77
breakdown - without cover	78
buying a car	99

C

cabriolet	33
caliper	16
camshaft	7,8,10,12
car dealership	55

D

T